Woody De Othello

Woody De Othello
Maybe tomorrow

Karma

Art and Inspiration in Woody De Othello's *Maybe tomorrow*

Jason R. Young

Maybe tomorrow takes its title from Grant Green's 1971 jazz recording of the same name. That song is a brooding rumination on the unfulfilled promises of the previous decade. Through a series of jaunty excursions and discordant chords, the song calls to mind the restive optimism that inaugurated the 1960s, while announcing the emergence of a new era, more languid and deliberate, more wearied and worn down.[1] Green's song is riddled with the blue notes of *saudade*—that ineffable feeling of nostalgia, melancholy, and loss for a love or person or freedom that will forever remain just out of reach. The echoes of that song, and of its sentiments, continue to reverberate. They reemerged as a sample at the heart of Kendrick Lamar's 2012 release "Sing About Me, I'm Dying of Thirst," a long, circuitous recording that rolls, Cadillac-style, through the streets of Los Angeles.[2] Lamar stands aside in "Sing About Me," taking on the posture of an unassuming bystander who nevertheless serves as vessel and mouthpiece, the voice of a new generation's caustic demands for recognition and redress. *Promise that you will sing about me.*

In Woody De Othello's 2022 exhibition *Maybe tomorrow*, these earlier reverberations are evident in an otherworldly gallery punctuated by dense, saturated hues. In a series of related mise-en-scènes, Othello offers a vision of (an)other, parallel world in which the familiar becomes foreign. Here, a faucet bends backward in a contorted remembrance of itself (*Faucet*, 2022). In this twisted, craning gesture, the faucet's neck recalls a *Sankofa*, an Akan-derived ideogram that has since been adopted and elaborated throughout the African diaspora. Sankofa is often associated with the Twi proverb *Se wo were fi na wosankofa a yenkyi* (It is not wrong to go back for that which you have forgotten). As

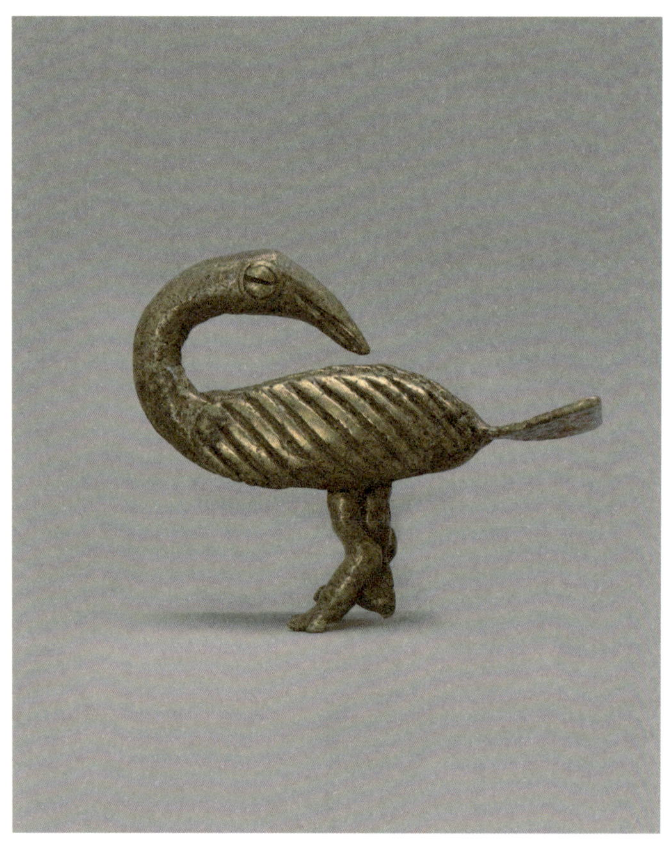

Akan gold weight in form of Sankofa bird, n.d. Brass, 1 × 2¾ × 1¼ in. (2.5 × 7 × 3.2 cm). Brooklyn Museum; Carll H. de Silver Fund

Kwame Anthony Appiah notes, Sankofa, and the larger body of Adinkra visual symbols of which it is a part, constitute a way of "supporting the transmission of a complex and nuanced body of practice and belief without writing."[3] Indeed, *Maybe tomorrow* is replete with visual puns whose power is rooted in their ability to evoke, remind, or hint at meanings that exceed the limits of the physical form. To take but one example, water emerges as a consistent theme throughout the exhibition, evoked in the form of faucets, fountains, and pools as well as in acts of cleansing, crossing, and drinking. For its part, Sankofa stands as both an instruction and an invocation for African peoples who crossed the waters to cast their gaze ever forward, making sure never to forget the past.

This persistent call to return to oneself constitutes a defining element in *Maybe tomorrow*. A kneeling figure atop a drum-shaped pedestal bows forward to reveal a long, tubular neck protruding out as an infinite fountain pouring of itself into its own basin (*Pouring into Self*, 2022). This sense of perpetually returning into one's self is further elaborated in the form of a kneeling figure in a penitent posture, oversized hands and long, bended feet emphasizing the power of the prayer (*On My Way Home*, 2022). Another figure assumes the lotus position high atop a stepladder. Here, nirvana is presented as akin to climbing stairs (*exhalation and praises*, 2022). A tall podium upholds another figure that in turn supports a powered light bulb under a volcano-shaped lampshade (*Keeping the light on*, 2022). In these acts of turning, twisting, bowing, and bending, Othello offers avenues to power—divine, earthly, electric— that promise the possibility of redress. Bright glazes render these figures in brilliant hues of subterranean brown, metallic midnight, fiery orange, and ocean blue. Despite their brilliance, these surfaces reveal remarkable texture and depth.

In addition to offering various means of turning inward, *Maybe tomorrow* also gestures to the past. In *Secrets Safe* (2002), Othello presents a large ceramic pot, emblazoned with a bright orange glaze, sitting atop a wooden pedestal. This vessel is reminiscent of the antebellum stoneware industry of Edgefield, South Carolina, where enslaved and newly freed African American potters toiled as a crucial part of the region's expansive ceramic tradition. Othello contributed a ceramic vessel (*Applying Pressure*, 2021) to *Hear Me Now: The Black Potters of Old Edgefield, South Carolina,* a wide-ranging exhibition at the Metropolitan Museum of Art, New York, that considered the historical production of nineteenth-century African American potters in dialogue with contemporary African American ceramicists.[4] *Applying Pressure* is comprised of various body parts—hands, ears, mouth, and lips—that come together to create an abstracted face vessel that recalls the Edgefield tradition.

Numerous ears are positioned in various poses throughout the body of *Secrets Safe.* They serve as auditory portals, connecting the dark, cavernous inside of the vessel to the world of sight and sound circulating outside. The title of the object operates as a double entendre. The vessel is, in one sense, a safe—a repository for the spoken and heard knowledge hiding within its clay walls; of its oral traditions, mother wit, counsel, and caution. But more than mere vault, *Secrets Safe* connotes a sacred trust, a collection of ingenuity, innovation, and skill passed from generation to generation, whispered from lip to lobe. Throughout *Maybe tomorrow*, Othello limns a physical landscape punctuated by dissociated body parts. Here, an ear, a mouth, an arm, a neck; there, a set of sharpened fingernails situated at the business end of a three-tined cultivator made for digging in garden soil. In these applications of body parts to the clay body, Othello invests these objects with the evidence of their making.

In one sense, *Maybe tomorrow* reflects the malaise of the modern. In *Prying and Prayer* (2022), the ceramic form of a column radiator with an analog desk phone perched on top assumes a prominent place in the gallery. This multilayered piece is full of surprises.

A pair of glistening ceramic praying hands is secreted into the center of the radiator. Ceramic ears laze about the body of the telephone. *Prying and Prayer* alludes to the noisy hisses, clicks, and hums that characterize column radiators with all of their air and water whooshing through tubes and valves. This and other artifacts of former technological innovations persist in this alternate world. A telephone receiver, a clunky remote control, and an analog clock radio can all be seen in various places. These objects reveal both their obsolescence as well as their persistence, as in the abstracted form of a light switch mounted against a bright-green wall (*Keep on keepin on*, 2022). These devices are as pedestrian as they are essential, each and all a persistent intrusion of old forms into this, the gilded immateriality of modern life. In drawing attention to everyday forms, Othello encourages a reckoning with modernity's reliance on—even celebration of—planned obsolescence.

If *Maybe tomorrow* is a meditation on the nature of modernity, it also exists in a time outside the normal, linear passage of hours, days, and years. A wall-mounted ceramic calendar is opened to a June whose days number thirty-one (*Faith in June*, 2022). An analog clock is mounted on a wall with numbers that traverse the face in counterclockwise fashion (*Follow me*, 2022). More timepieces appear on a nightstand (*Morning light*, 2022) and atop a pedestal (*Every last drop*, 2022), each one indicating different times of day. Writing in *Invisible Man*, Ralph Ellison chronicles the curious passage of time for Black people:

Invisibility, let me explain, gives one a slightly different sense of

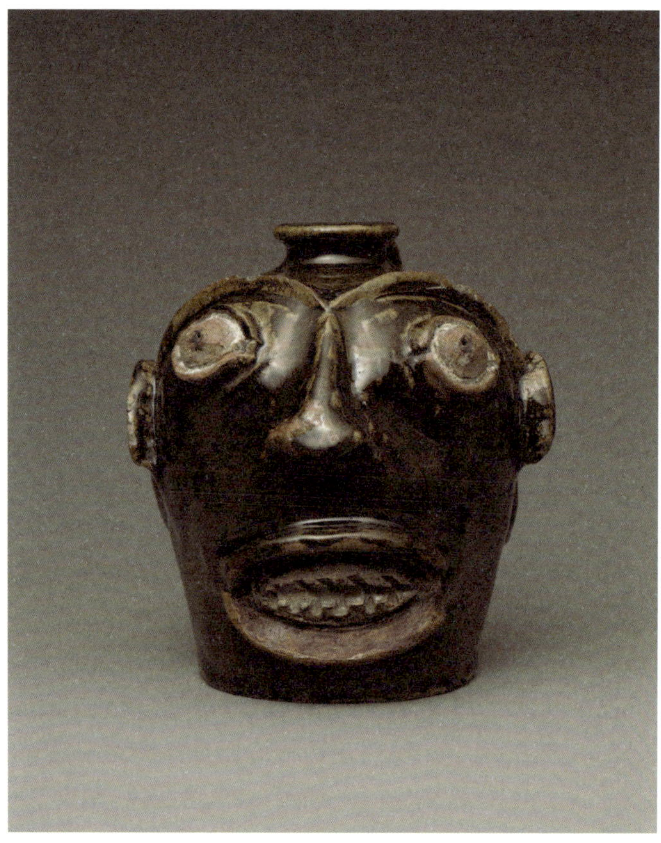

Face jug, ca. 1850–80, unrecorded Edgefield district potter (American), Alkaline-glazed stoneware with kaolin, 5⅞ in. (14.9 cm) height. Metropolitan Museum of Art, New York; purchase, Friends of the American Wing Fund and Alvia Baker Gift, in honor of Derrick Beard

the past onto the present."[6] In this view, the imperative of Black Time emerges from its persistent repetition, "its looping and determined return, [by which] black Atlantic subjectivities are able . . . to be seen."[7] Much like Ellison's protagonist in *Invisible Man*, Brown suggests that Black people are "simultaneously hypervisible and invisible," flickering subjectivities who reverberate through the centuries.[8] In this way, *Maybe tomorrow* eschews any simple return to or recapitulation of past forms. Instead, the instability of Black Time is reflected in *Maybe tomorrow* in the inherent fluidity, movement, and melting of objects that continue to "slip into the breaks."

Despite the dour discussions that so often attend the artistic production of Black artists, I think it important to revel in the joy and fluidity of an exhibition that insists on the power of a place not here and a time not now. Writing in reference to a related topic, art historian Yvonne Patricia Chireau turns our attention to the primacy of *delight* at the heart of African diasporic expression:

> time, you're never quite on the beat. Sometimes you're ahead and sometimes behind. Instead of the swift and imperceptible flowing of time, you are aware of its nodes, those points where time stands still or from which it leaps ahead. And you slip into the breaks and look around.[5]

> Delight. What a word. What a concept. So instead of the terror of chaos being overcome with a map that provides us with order by fixing our location, we have the messiness of lack of fit. We have the possibilities for transcendence and play, delight, frivolity . . . in the movement, departure from sequence, leap away from linearity, playful disturbance, to jump from order to disorder and returning again . . . [in] the freedom of play.[9]

In this sense, the brassy ceramic trumpet that appears in *Maybe tomorrow* reflects a further elaboration of timekeeping that is so central to this exhibition. In describing the uncanny nature of "Black Time," Kimberly Juanita Brown insists on "the temporal instability that weaves

From this, Chireau queries, "What could be more African in some essentialized sense than a perspective that privileges self-aware play as

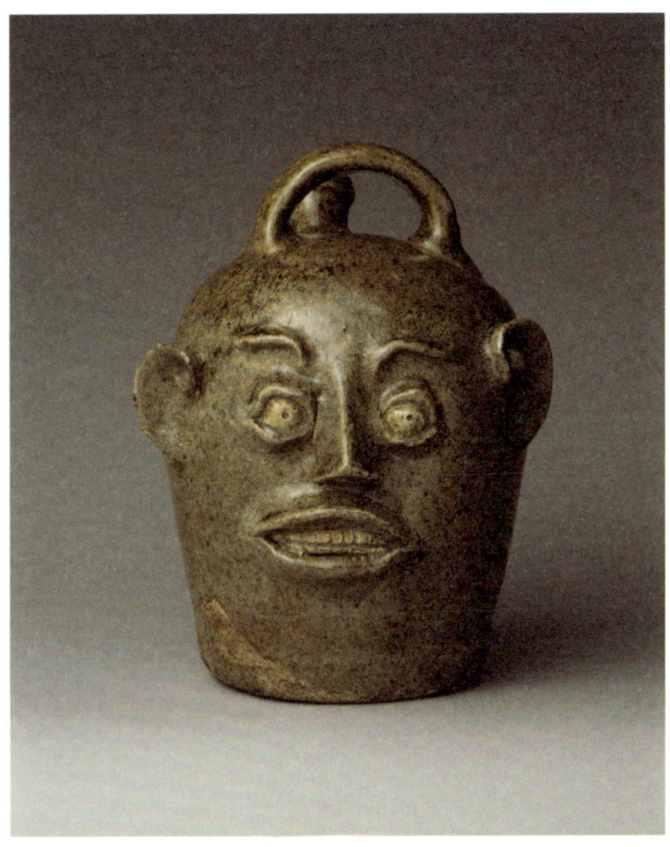

Face jug, ca. 1850–80, unrecorded Edgefield district potter (American). Alkaline-glazed stoneware with kaolin, 10¼ in. (26 cm) height. Metropolitan Museum of Art, New York; purchase, Nancy Dunn Revocable Trust Gift

an aesthetic that might govern the very serious work" of Black cultural, religious, and artistic expression?[10] In building out an alternate, otherworldly space in *Maybe tomorrow*, Othello opens new possibilities for the here and now. If the exhibition presents a world unto itself, it still provides several avenues of escape from or for communion in our own here and now. A mounted ceramic vent connotes the free movement of air in and out of the space, the grille-face reminiscent of a pair of breathing lungs (*Bone broth*, 2022). Ceramic knobs affixed to the door suggest both locking and unlocking, entering and exiting, the free flow of people across the door's threshold, and a border checkpoint to keep "others" out.

Writing in *Scenes of Subjection*, Saidiya Hartman describes "insurgent nostalgia" as a set of "sacralized and ancestral elements" that Black people create in their attempts to "remember things they have not witnessed or experienced."[11] One thinks here of bottle trees and inverted pots, white kaolin and Georgia red clay. The ultimate witnessing that emerges from this nostalgia "has little or nothing to do with the veracity of recollection or the reliability or fallibility of memory."[12] Instead, the very act of remembering—the embrace of an insurgent nostalgia—constitutes a demand for redress rather than a mere "inventory of memory."[13] *Maybe tomorrow* comprises just this sort of witnessing. A small ceramic figure of a dog holds court in the middle of this exhibition, seeing all through the rounded absences that serve as eyes, hearing all through two humanlike ears (*Sentient sunshine*, 2022). *Promise that you will sing about me.*

NOTES

1. Grant Green, "Maybe Tomorrow," track 2 on *Visions*, Blue Note BST 84373, 1971, 33⅓ rpm.
2. Kendrick Lamar, "Sing About Me, I'm Dying of Thirst," track 10 on *good kid, m.A.A.d city*, Aftermath Entertainment/Interscope B0017534-02, 2012, compact disc.
3. Kwame Anthony Appiah, *In My Father's House: Africa in the Philosophy of Culture* (London: Methuen, 1992), 132–33.
4. *Hear Me Now: The Black Potters of Old Edgefield, South Carolina*, Metropolitan Museum of Art, New York, September 9, 2022–February 5, 2023.
5. Ralph Ellison, *Invisible Man* (New York: Random House, 1982), 8.
6 Kimberly Juanita Brown, *The Repeating Body: Slavery's Visual Resonance in the Contemporary* (Durham, NC: Duke University Press, 2015), 17.
7. Ibid.
8. Ibid.
9. S. A. Khabeer, Yvonne Patricia Chireau, and P. C. Johnson, "Mapping Africana Religions: Transnationalism, Globalization, and Diaspora," *Journal of Africana Religions* 2, no. 1 (2014): 133.
10. Ibid.
11. Saidiya V. Hartman, *Scenes of Subjection: Terror, Slavery, and Self-Making in Nineteenth-Century America* (New York: Oxford University Press, 1997), 72–73.
12. Ibid.
13. Ibid.

Woody De Othello in Conversation with Allie Biswas

ALLIE BISWAS: There are certain motifs that have come to be associated with your work. For instance, you often make sculptures of clocks and telephones, or vases that incorporate human features. Given this process of repetition—of your interest in exploring a specific iconography—how do you decide what kind of object you are going to focus on when it comes to making a new sculpture?

WOODY DE OTHELLO: I'm thinking about the context of the universe of the work, as I would describe it. If I'm working toward an exhibition, I'll think about how the different objects are interacting with each other. So my decision-making will come from that place: How do I establish this sense of range, of objects that are contradicting or offering something different from one another? I also want to expand my vocabulary, so I'm always trying to search

for objects that can communicate some type of metaphor. I think that a lot of the objects I gravitate toward are metaphors for bigger things in life. Referencing shoes and sandals and feet—to me, that's all about forward movement and progression.

ALLIE BISWAS: There is a clarity in your sculptures that I think is reflective of your interest in expressing universal conditions— namely, how to navigate momentum, or, even more so, a lack of impetus in our daily lives.

WOODY DE OTHELLO: It's all very simple. And that simplicity is a way of communicating that makes sense to me. I don't want things to be convoluted or too detached. I didn't necessarily grow up with an art history background, going to museums. My knowledge of contemporary art is still very fresh. So I think the things that I gravitate toward just make sense on this

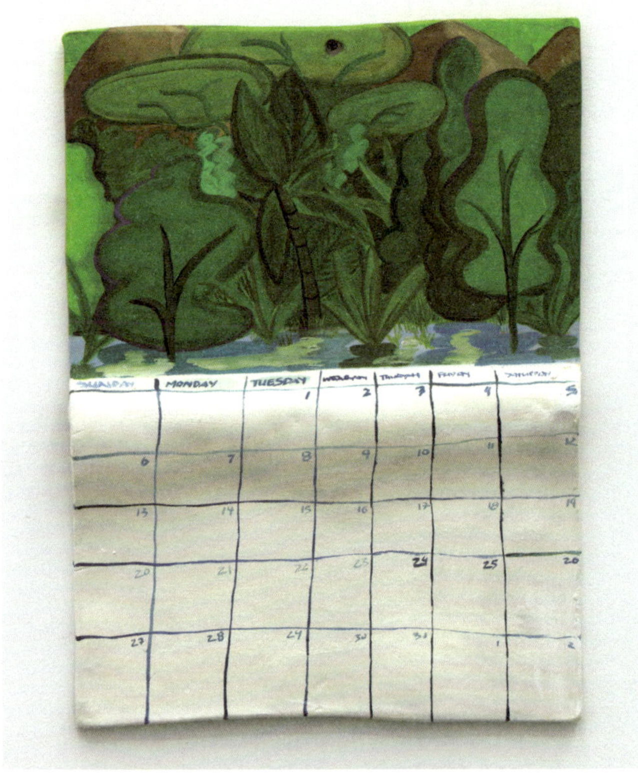

Woody De Othello, *Faith in June*, 2022. Ceramic and paint, 19 × 14½ × 1½ in. (48.3 × 36.8 × 3.8 cm)

quintessential human level. What do people have encounters with? For me, that starts off with referencing things that are recognizable.

ALLIE BISWAS: With *Maybe tomorrow*, several of your sculptures were arranged as a group, which gave the impression that they belong together, as one unit. The way that the exhibition was designed emphasizes this, because it's a separate room with its own door, detached from the rest of the gallery. Is it important to you that the sculptures are shown, or even just considered, as a group, rather than as individual works?

WOODY DE OTHELLO: When I'm in the studio, I'm working on multiple things at a time. My studio ethos is to add opposites

or contradictions; things that are formally separate from each other. I'm always looking to make a body of work or an exhibition that feels very full, so the individual features can't be stagnant. I've been homing in on this idea for the past couple of years—of creating objects that feel like they're very much *inside*—and I think that *Maybe tomorrow* at Karma has been, to this day, the most successful execution of that process.

ALLIE BISWAS: So you're considering the interior space, like a room within your house, but also something that feels very personal and close to you.

WOODY DE OTHELLO: *Inside* means something internal, something private, something intimate. I feel like there are different ways to communicate the idea of being in your body or inside of your head, mentally. Right now, using these domestic spaces is a way for me to get at that idea.

ALLIE BISWAS: The exhibition at Karma introduced new motifs, such as the calendar and birds, other ways to consider space and time.

WOODY DE OTHELLO: Those objects are very new. I didn't start making the birds until 2022 and I feel like part of what I'm trying to do is to force myself out of my comfort zone. Now, I'm thinking: What is the opposite of this interior space? So, little elements from the outside are starting to make themselves known. *Faith in June* (2022), again, is one of these very direct references to time, but the actual image of the calendar is a landscape of this imagined outdoor scene. I'm trying to think about ways to, again, expand. To push myself in the studio, to be a little bit uncomfortable.

ALLIE BISWAS: So you're conscious of wanting to develop your work, so that it doesn't become stagnant to you?

WOODY DE OTHELLO: I want my work to feel like this thing that has the potential to be expansive and, at least for me, freeing. Something important about making art is to be able to find freedom. A part of that is taking steps in a direction that you can't even really plan out. The dog is also very new.

ALLIE BISWAS: Your dog was your lockdown hero during the pandemic.

WOODY DE OTHELLO: Exactly. And dogs are kind of unbelievable. It's been a transformative experience. That creature offers so much through nonverbal communication and that has been truly life-changing. The bird sculptures also came from me having my dog. She will look up at birds flying in the sky. And the birds—that symbolism of looking up—I think that's a sign of optimism as well.

ALLIE BISWAS: Let's talk about the role played by the human body in your work. When you were studying for your master's at California College of the Arts in San Francisco, you made a series of figures that you exhibited in specific public spaces, such as the barber shop and the bodega.

WOODY DE OTHELLO: As an undergrad, I was also making these life-sized ceramic figures.

ALLIE BISWAS: So when you started working with clay, you were focused on replicating the body in some way?

WOODY DE OTHELLO: Almost immediately. All of my drawings and 2-D work up to that point related to these kinds of stylized figures. They were creepy. They were weird. These "people" were obviously going through some type of internal distress and looking for ways to heal and cope. When I was showing this type of work, I would go to thrift stores and buy furniture. But there was something about placing the figure among the furniture that, to me, didn't completely mesh. It didn't feel like the objects belonged to the figures, and there was this sense of the objects not

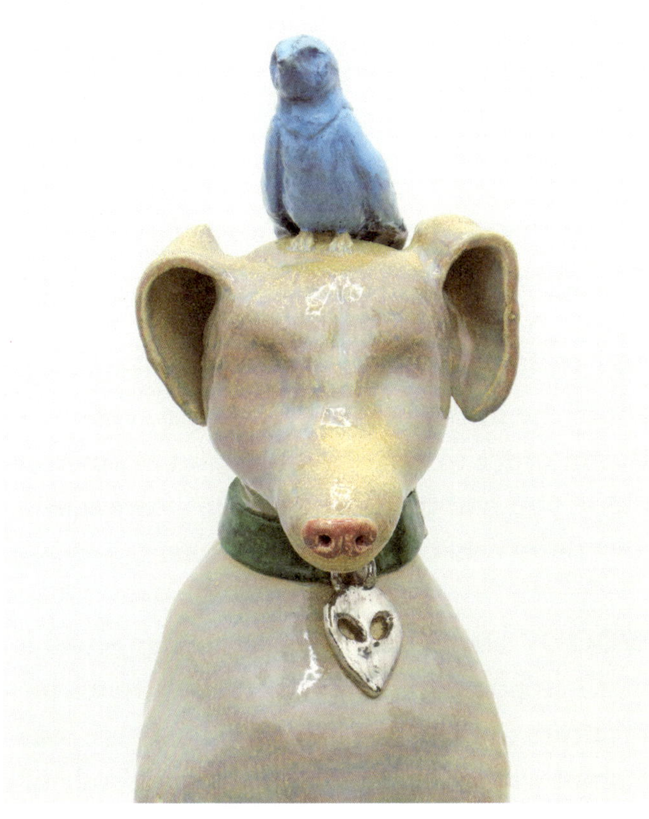

Woody De Othello, *Sentient sunshine*, 2022. Ceramic and glaze, 27 × 14 × 15 in. (68.6 × 35.7 × 38 cm)

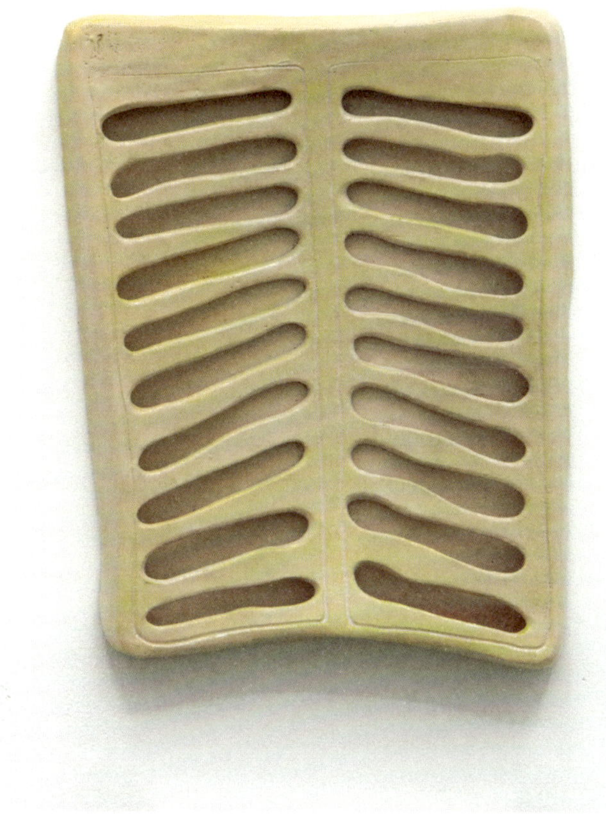

Woody De Othello, *Bone broth*, 2022. Ceramic and paint,
18 × 12 × 2 in. (45.7 × 30.5 × 5.1 cm)

having this quality of being really *lived in* by the figures I was creating.

ALLIE BISWAS: You were already thinking about the importance of creating a scene. But in order to establish that kind of environment, you had to remove the furniture and find these other communal spaces.

WOODY DE OTHELLO: What happened is that I stopped trying to collect these items of furniture to make the installations. There was a point where I had developed a little body of work of these figurative sculptures and I had put clothes on them. I took photos of them

against a white wall and integrated, through Photoshop, these different images from TV shows, movies, and other random photos I had found. That helped me to start moving past that initial dilemma. Then, I was just like, OK, the issue I'm having with this is about the texture of a space not being lived-in. I can't fabricate that in a gallery, so let me take these objects or these figures and put them in my apartment. Let me go to the barber shop or the bodega and photograph them there. So I photographed them in real-life places to pick up on this sense of what it is to live in a space. But, actually, that also didn't work for me.

ALLIE BISWAS: Why was that?

WOODY DE OTHELLO: It was just too much of a separation, right? The figures obviously felt like they were from another dimension or another world, so to try and fit them into these places like the barber shop didn't make sense.

ALLIE BISWAS: It was jarring.

WOODY DE OTHELLO: Exactly. There was just such a dichotomy there. So, somewhere along the line, transitioning into graduate school, I was just like, all right, well, what happens if I start to make the objects themselves? I had been photographing these figurative sculptures in real spaces in graduate school, but it wasn't quite right. It still felt unresolved. It was a little bit too didactic and straightforward: what you see is what you get. None of it was really working out. I realized that what I needed to do was to try and make sculptures of the objects that the figures had been placed within. And that's what kind of opened this whole can of worms.

ALLIE BISWAS: When we spoke earlier in the year, you talked about domestic spaces as "containers for psychic energy." Was this the moment when you started to think about your surroundings in that way?

WOODY DE OTHELLO: I think that kind of logic and way of thinking came in graduate school. I remember reading *Phenomenology of Perception* by Maurice Merleau-Ponty. In one chapter, he talks about the body as a form of perception and that got me thinking about how our bodies interact with objects. I think that's when I made the clear decision to stop making explicitly figurative stuff and instead think about the viewer as being the body in the work. And that opened up this idea of anthropomorphizing these things. I started to research the ways in which cultures and religions have anthropomorphized everyday objects.

ALLIE BISWAS: I know that you have a specific interest in Yoruba culture, as well as the pottery traditions of the American South.

WOODY DE OTHELLO: I came across face jugs. And from there, going back a little bit further, I came across the Yoruba religion and great African artworks. The objects were so imbued with a sense of spirituality. But they were also these performative things, not things that merely existed. They were used in tribal affairs. There are times when I have made something and then I find a reference to a precolonial object or a tradition that reaffirms the thing that I've made. For instance, I've been making these series of fans and air-conditioning units and air purifiers, and, for me, it was always an analogy for how these interior spaces

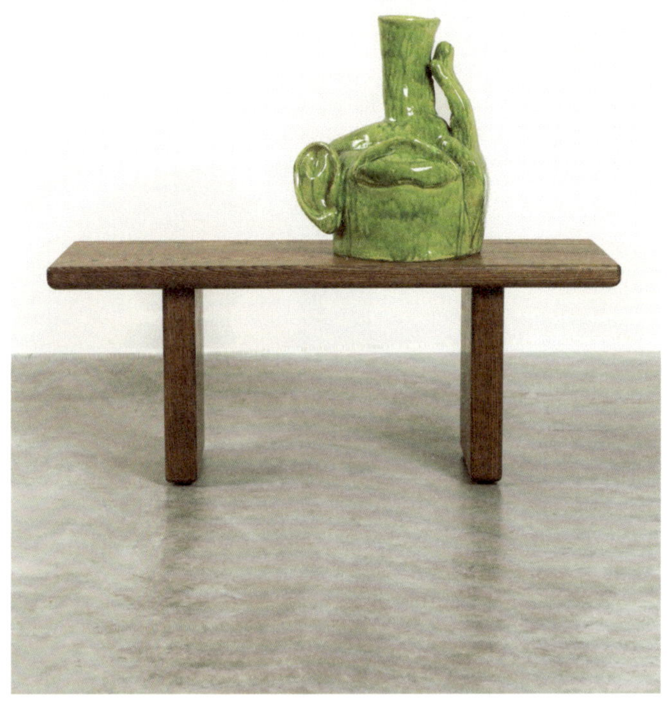

Woody De Othello, *Applying Pressure*, 2021. Ceramic, glaze, and red oak, 2 parts: 38 × 44 × 16 in. (96.5 × 111.8 × 40.6 cm) bench; 18 × 44 × 15 in. (45.7 × 111.8 × 38.1 cm) vessel; 19 × 16 × 15 in. (48.3 × 40.6 × 38.1 cm) overall

breathe. I was reading this book, *Art and Power*, which is about the Bantu Kingdom and their sculptural practice. They have a word which means air, breath, wind, and light force. This one word can encompass everything. I like how the way that I'm dealing with these things, at first glance, can be cheeky and just very surface level, but I feel like that's how you pull people into actually hearing what you have to say.

ALLIE BISWAS: It sounds as though the historical references you have cited were reached intuitively and organically, rather than something you deliberately wanted to

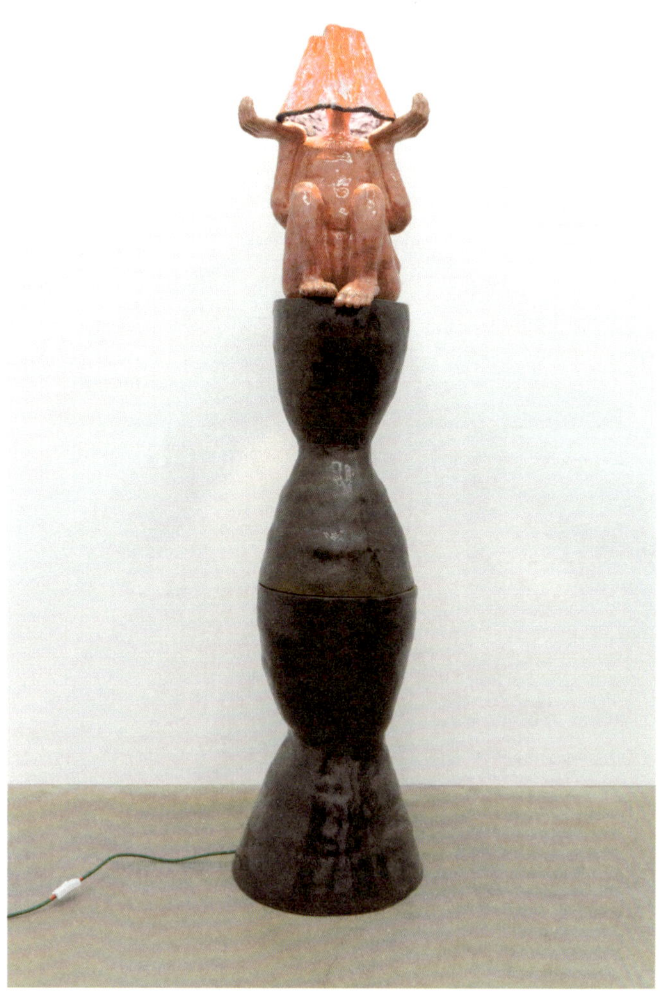

Woody De Othello, *Keeping the light on*, 2022. Ceramic, glaze, and lightbulb with wire, 70 × 20 × 20 in. (177.8 × 50.8 × 50.8 cm)

attach to your work. You have also discussed your interest in Haiti, where your parents grew up before moving to the United States, and I wonder if this inherited culture has also shaped your thinking to any extent?

WOODY DE OTHELLO: It's one of those things: it's not at the top of my mind, but it's in my heart and in my spirit. It's a part of how I maneuver. And I'm understanding the magnitude of that as I'm getting older and becoming more aware. I realize how the world

that's coming to me is tragic, but also that something new can be created. I'm thinking about Édouard Glissant, his book *Poetics of Relation*, where he talks about hybridity and creolization, and how colonization doesn't always need to be this form of erasure. I'm not trying to make it sound like it's something that isn't *just terrible*. But something does get created when you have different cultures coming together. And I look at Haiti as an example of that. I look at myself, a first-generation American, as something that's hard to make sense of, because I am Haitian, but I've never been to Haiti and I don't speak Creole. So I'm trying to grapple with what that means. My parents don't even have access to their history. I've never seen a photo of my grandparents. So much information has been lost. So not having access to these things, you have to create them, or somehow piece things together. And the way to do that is to ask, what do you have an affinity toward? What strikes you on an intimate, subconscious, bodily level? Those moments where you don't have any language for what that sensation is. I feel like making art and becoming more and more invested in the material of clay is helping me to find my way back to the past, but it's also how I'm maneuvering forward in life.

ALLIE BISWAS: Your sculptures were recently displayed in the exhibition *Hear Me Now: The Black Potters of Old Edgefield, South Carolina*, at the Metropolitan Museum of Art in New York, which added context to your work that is reflective of some of the things you have just been talking about.

WOODY DE OTHELLO: Being a part of that show at the Met, it's contextualizing all of that. I took my parents there, to not only show them that exhibition, but to also visit the Africa and Egypt exhibition [*The African Origin of Civilization*] and show them all of these artifacts. Even my dad, looking at these large vessels and containers, was like, "Oh, we had these in Haiti."

ALLIE BISWAS: The works that you make where the vessel is combined with the human feel distinct from the sculptures of representative household objects. But this is really more of a formal, stylistic distinction. It's not that your practice should be separated into these two categories, presented as opposites, because that would, of course, be missing the point.

WOODY DE OTHELLO: I was reading this book, *The New Black Gods*, which outlines all the Yoruba deities and their attributes. Ogun, for instance, is characterized by the material iron, but symbols of his presence include a comb, a gardening fork, and a shovel. I'm thinking, OK, so these everyday objects have the capacity to be metaphors and containers for other representations. It's just tapping into that space a little bit more. Looking at the different ways that diasporic cultures mourn their dead, oftentimes they will bring an object that reminds them of the person to the gravesite. The human sculptures I make are very much related to the other works; I don't think about them as separate. I think about them all as reaffirming each other.

Maybe tomorrow

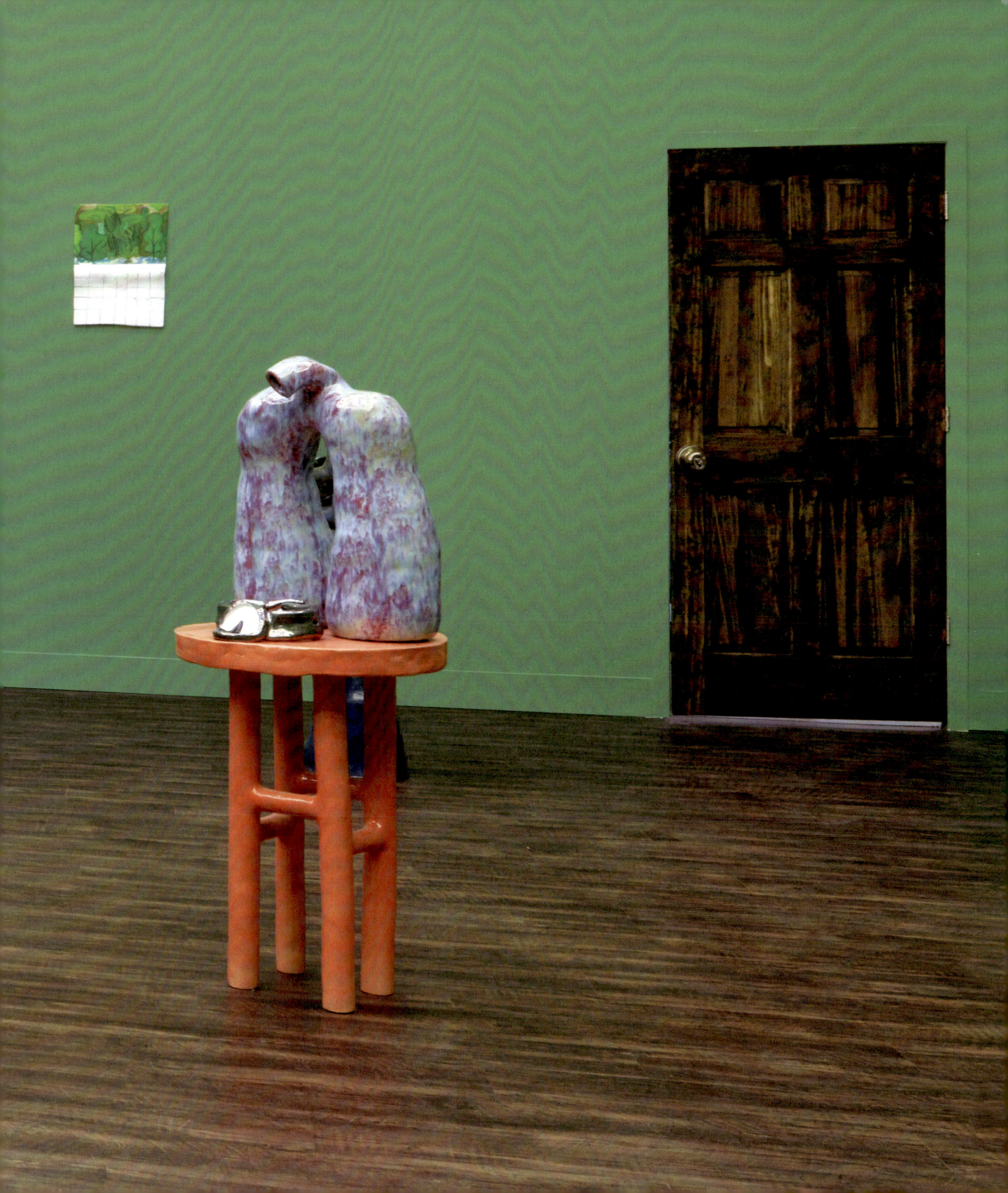

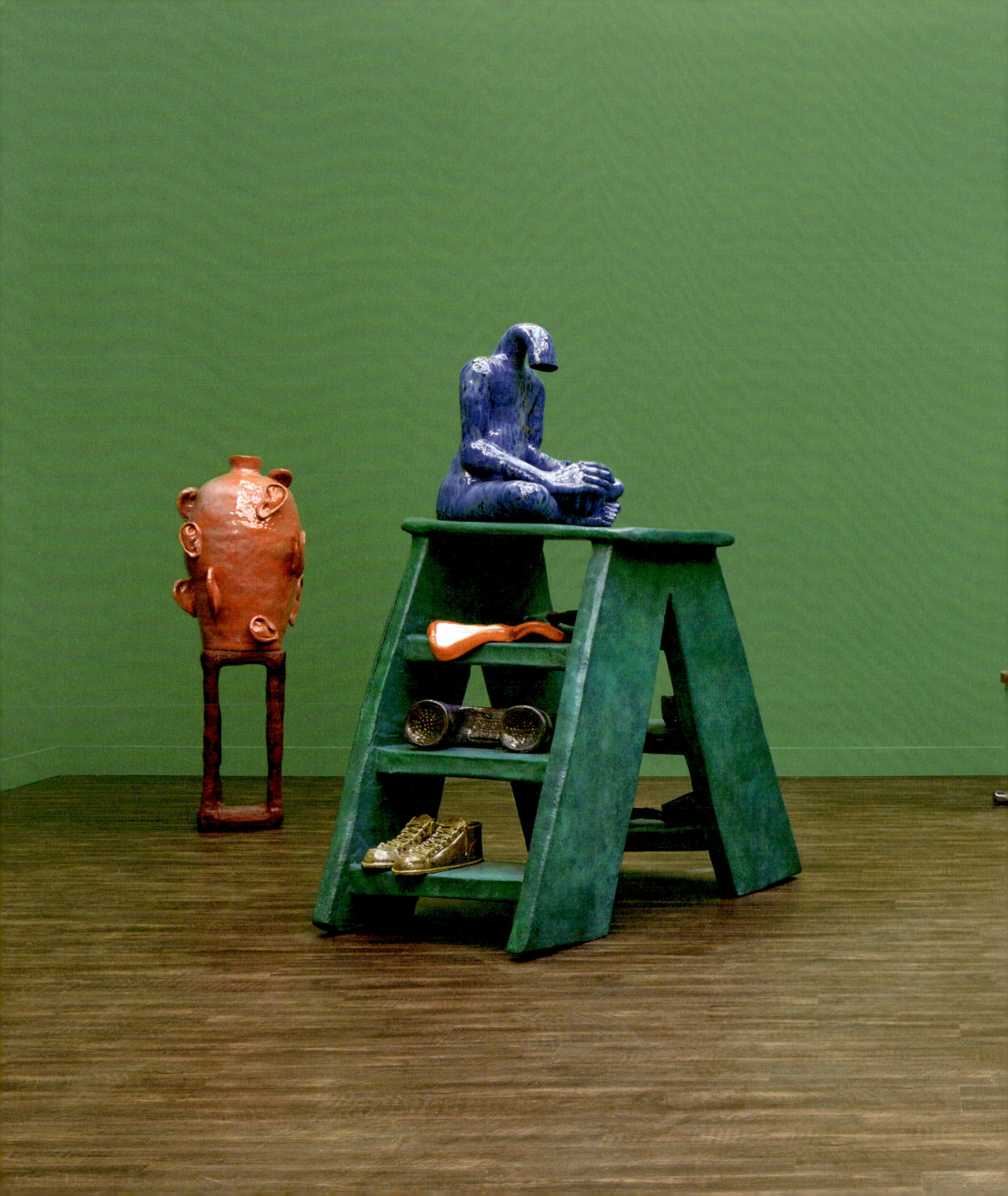

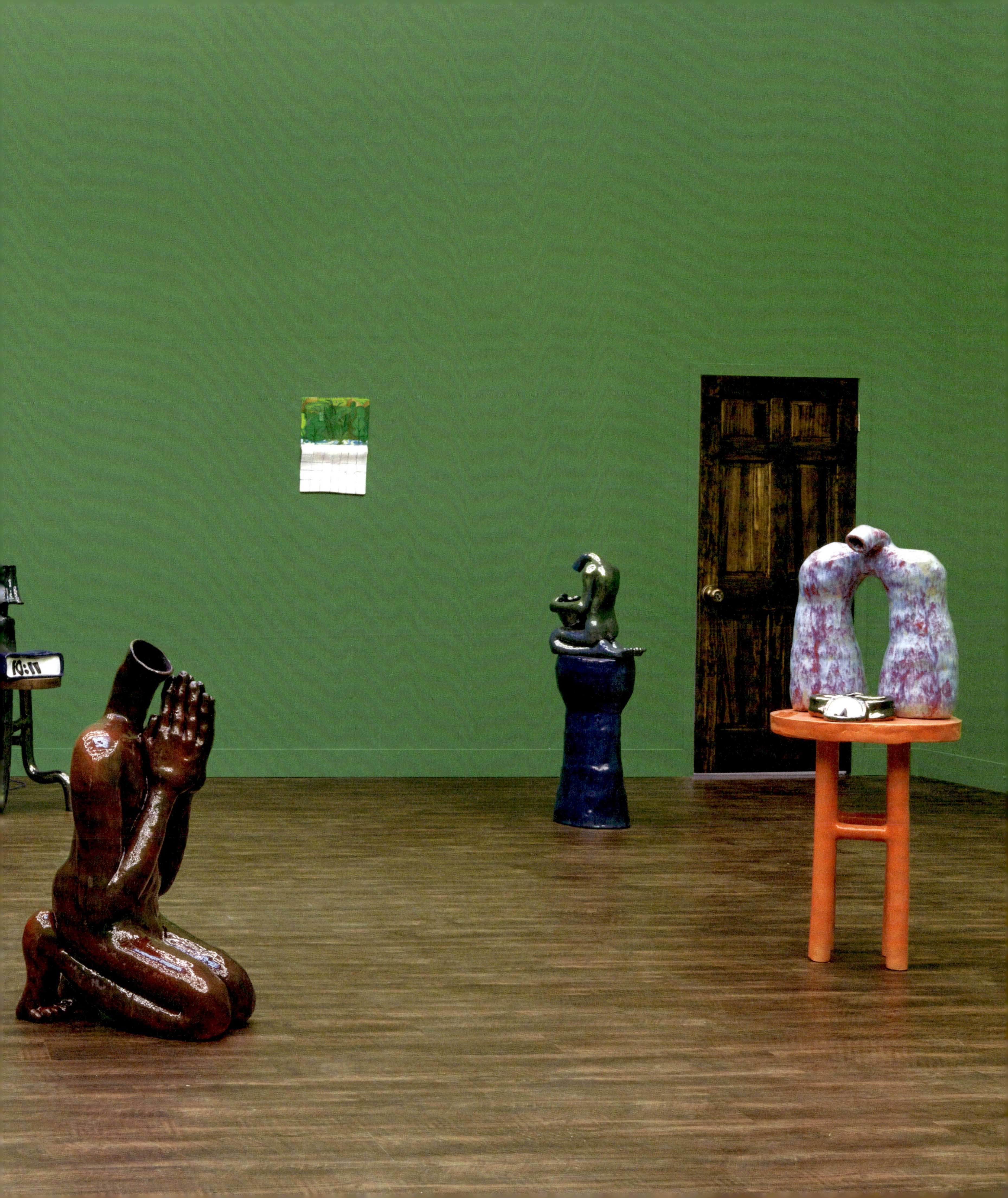

Pouring into self, 2022. Ceramic and glaze,
48 × 20 × 20 in. (121.9 × 50.8 × 50.8 cm)

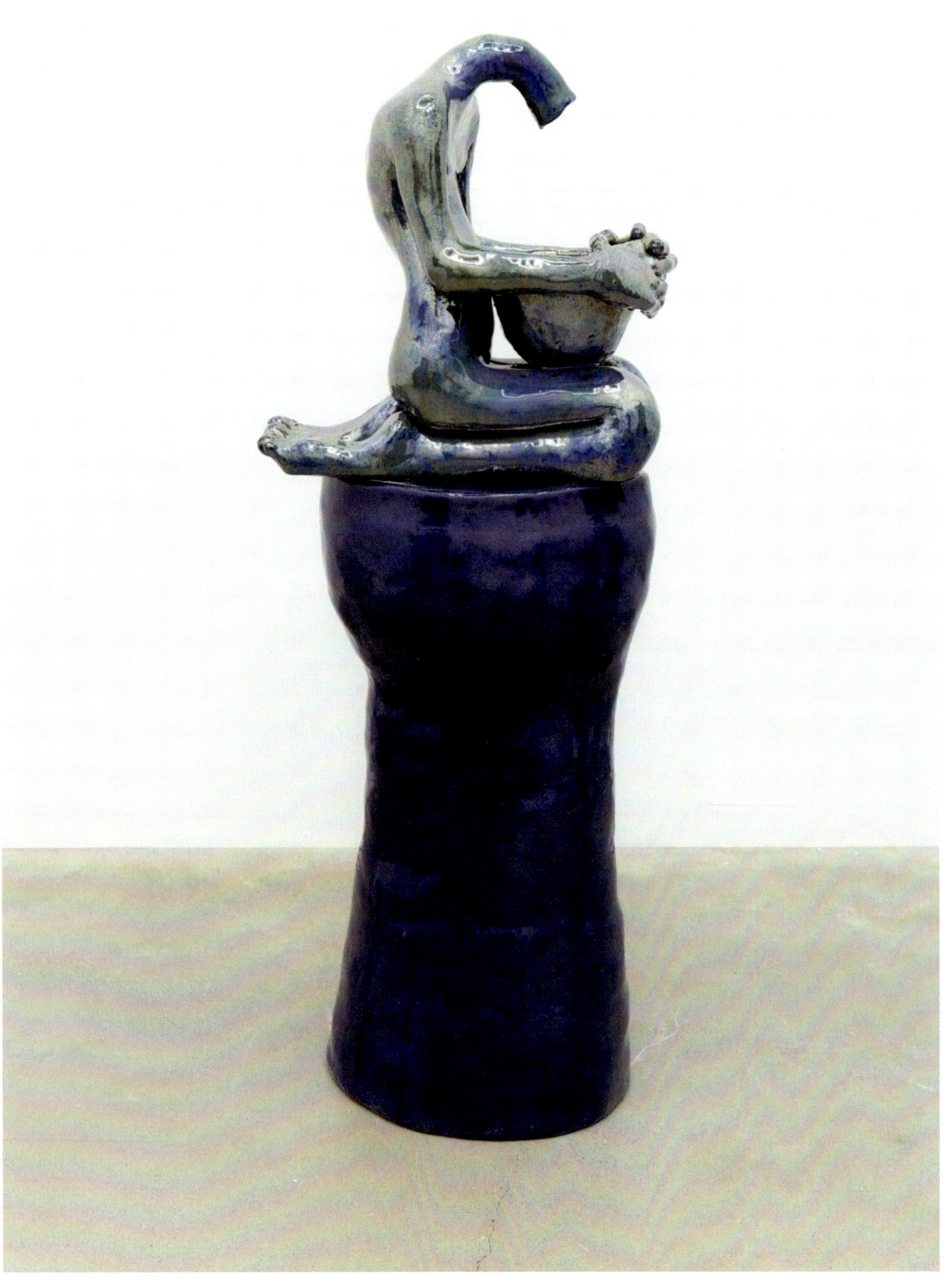

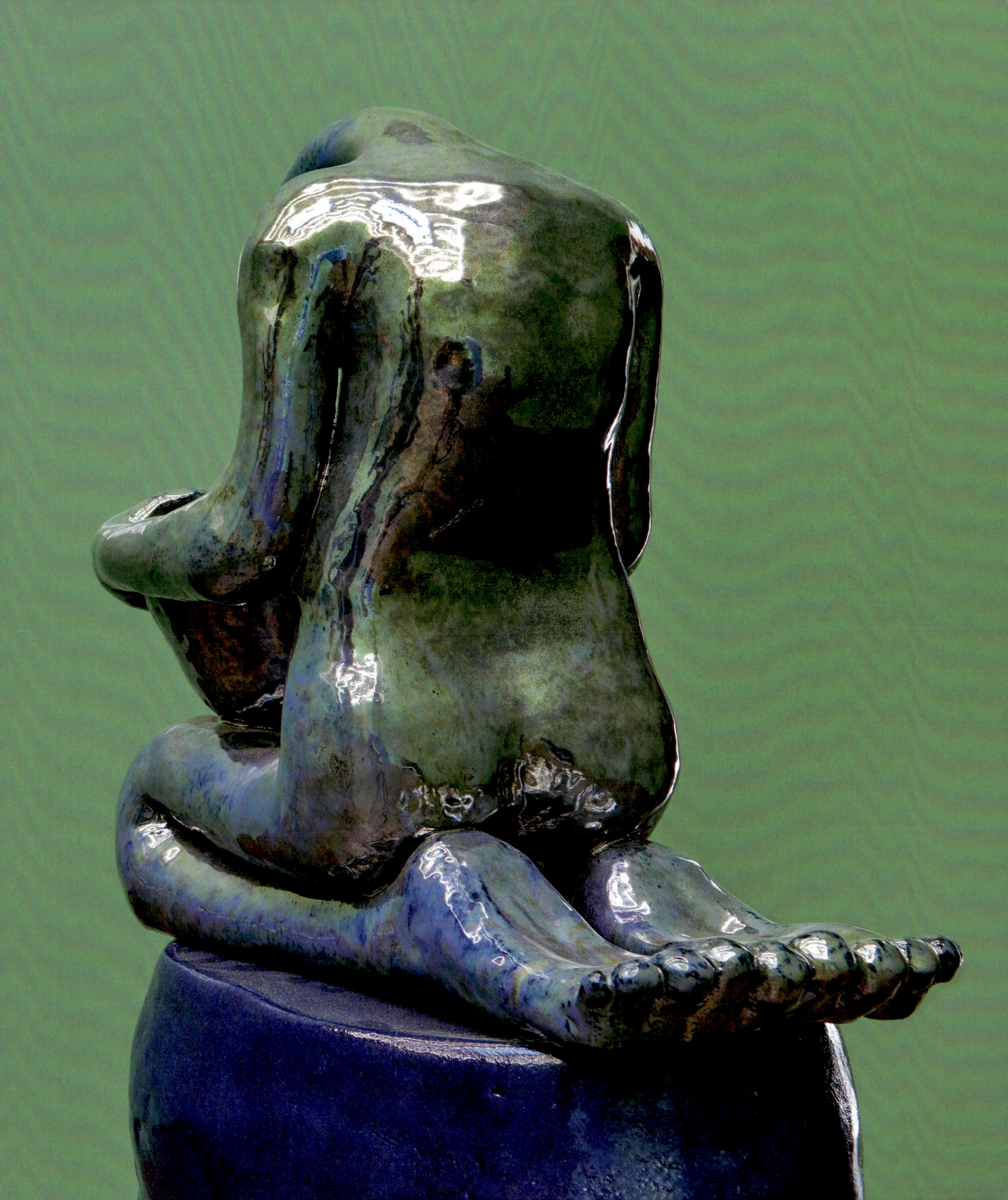

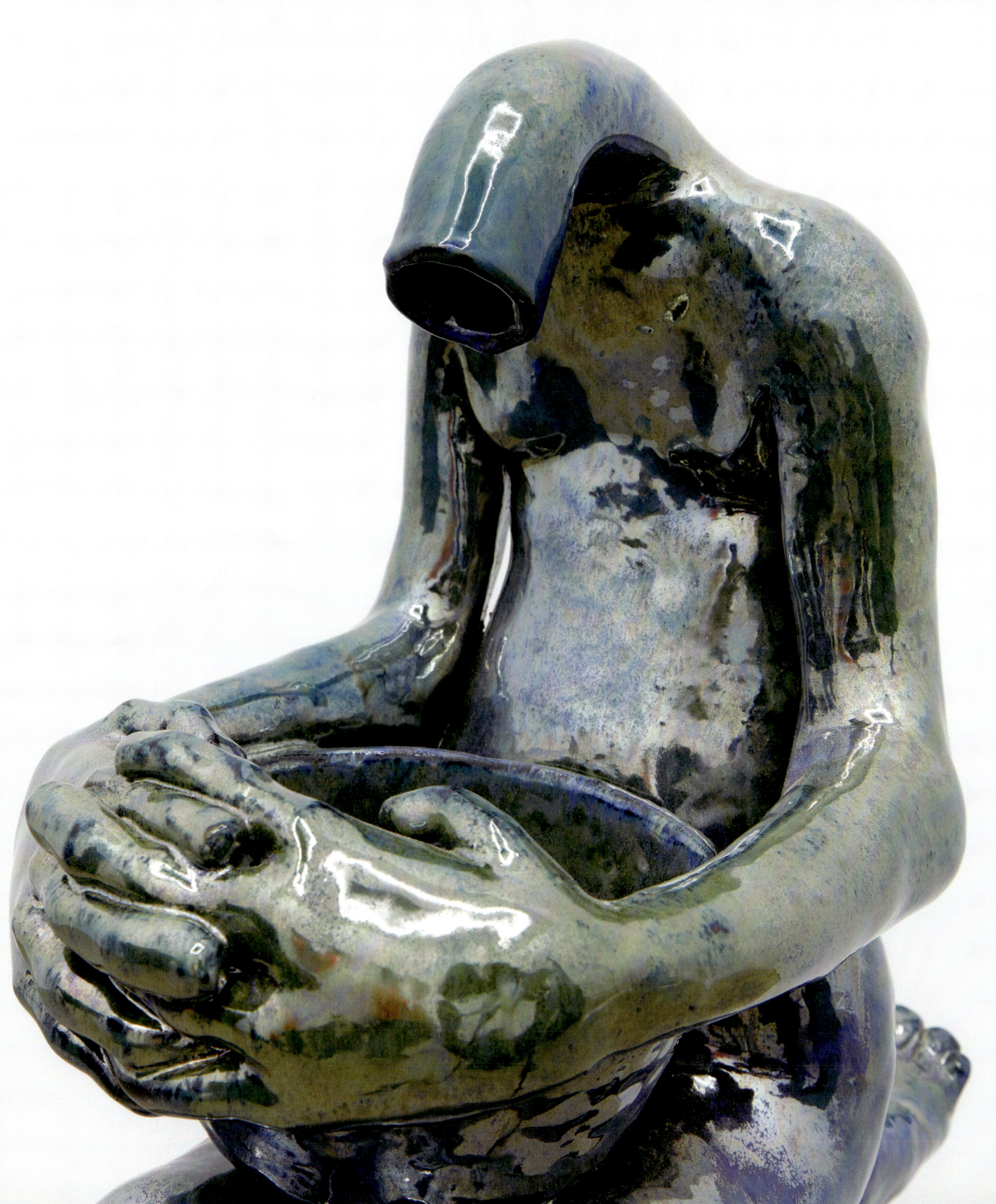

Untitled (Doorknob), 2022. Ceramic and glaze,
5 × 5 × 5 in. (12.7 × 12.7 × 12.7 cm)

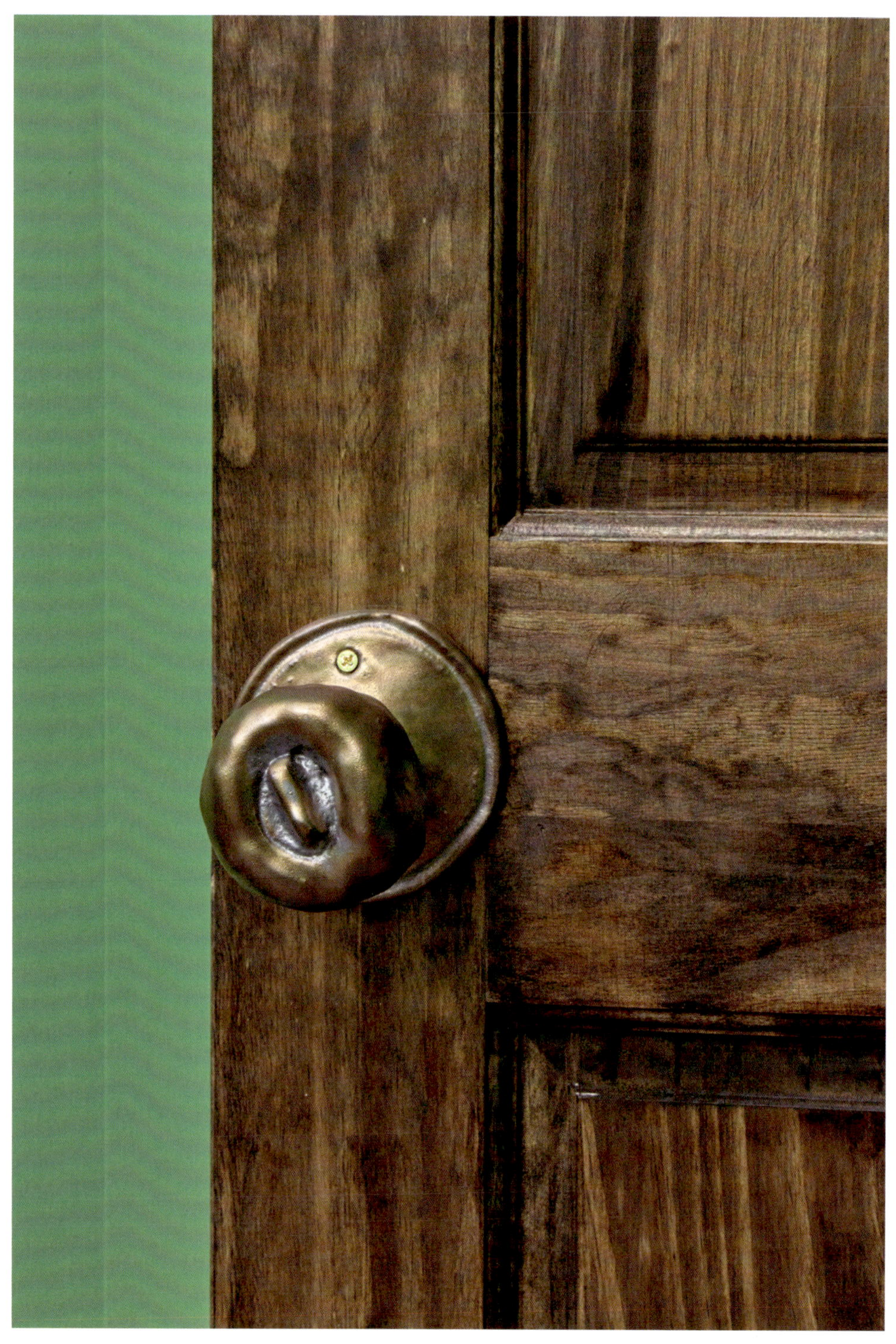

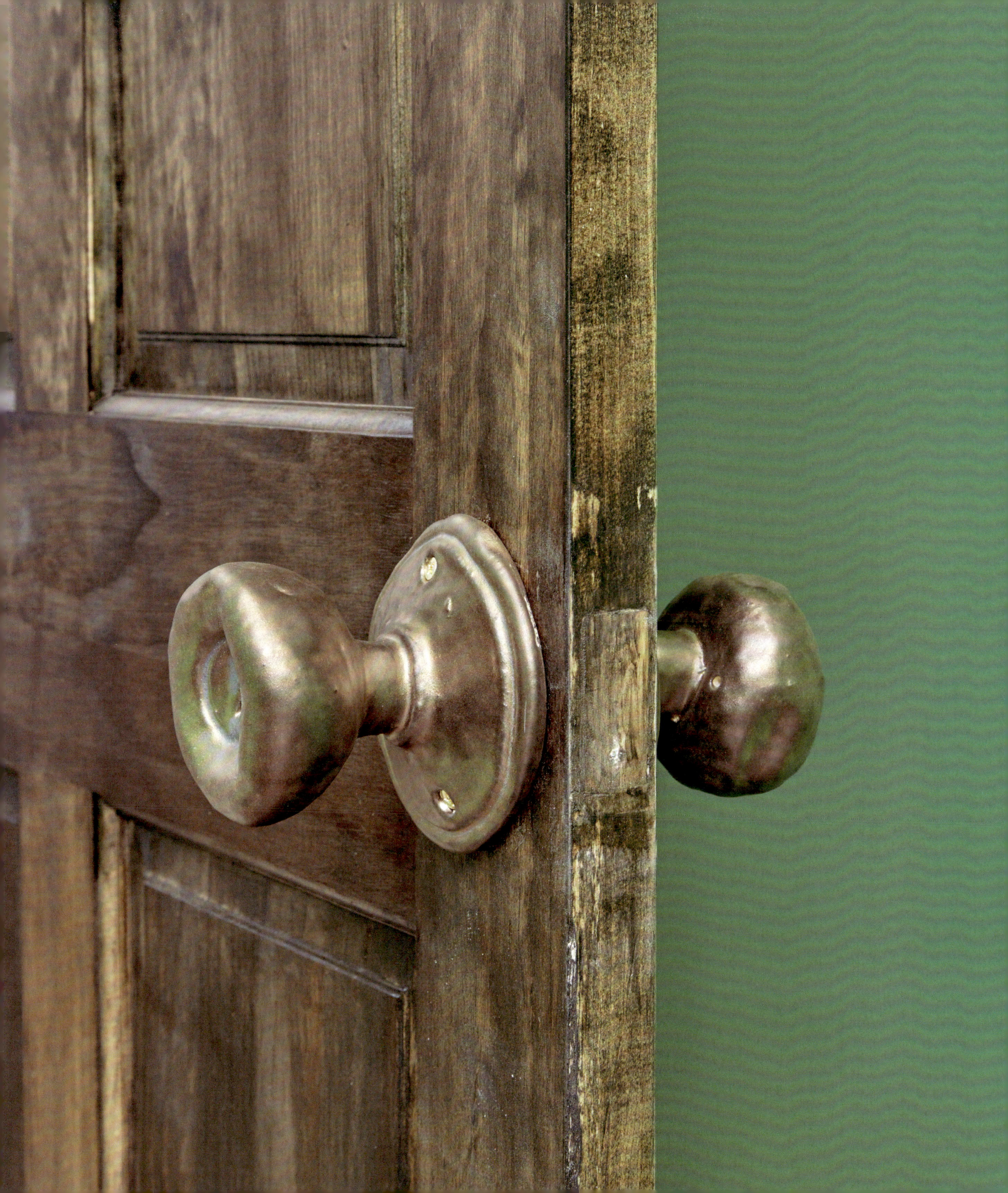

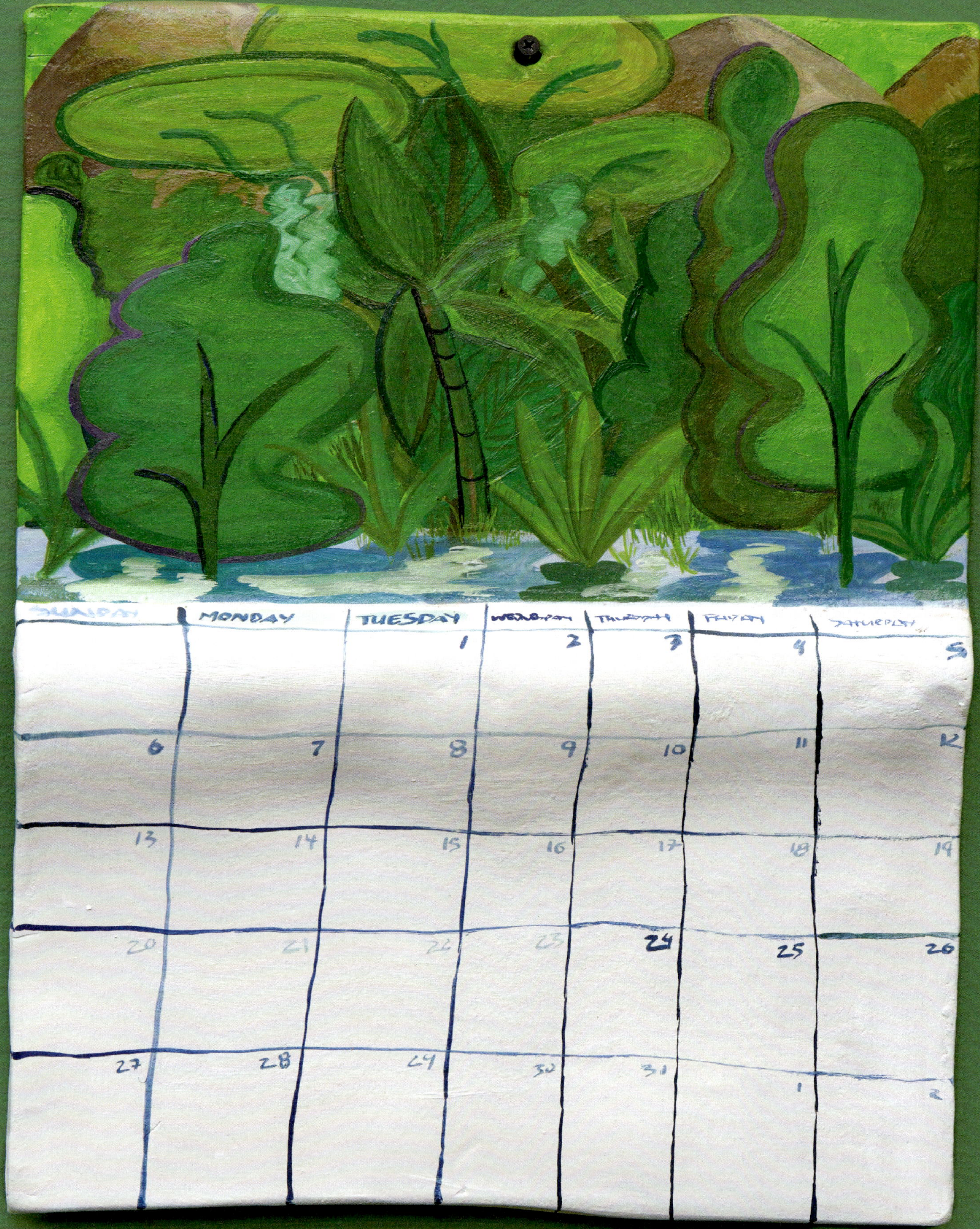

SUNDAY MONDAY TUESDAY WEDNESDAY THURSDAY FRIDAY SATURDAY
1 2 3 4 5
6 7 8 9 10 11 12
13 14 15 16 17 18 19
20 21 22 23 24 25 26
27 28 29 30 31 1 2

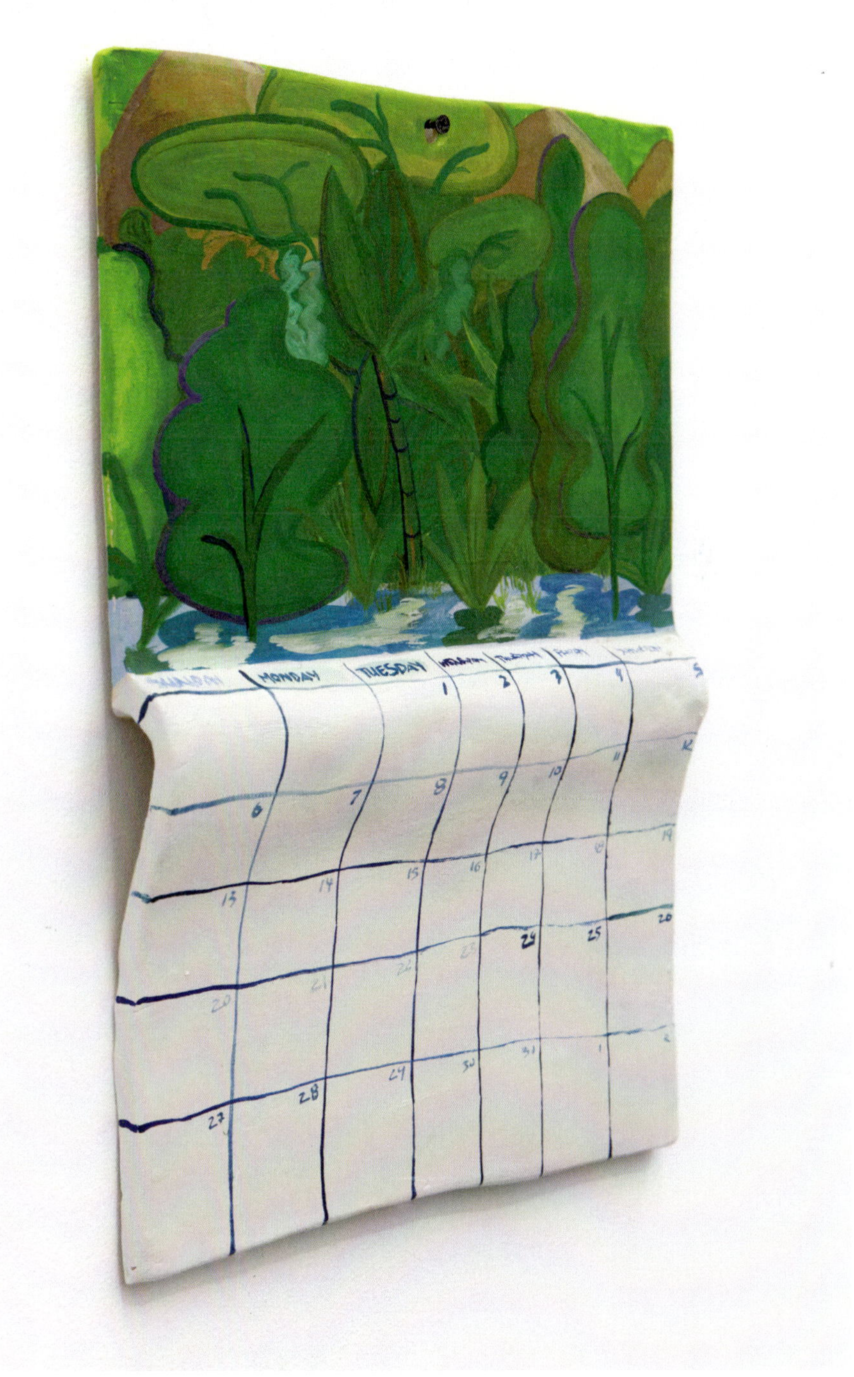

35

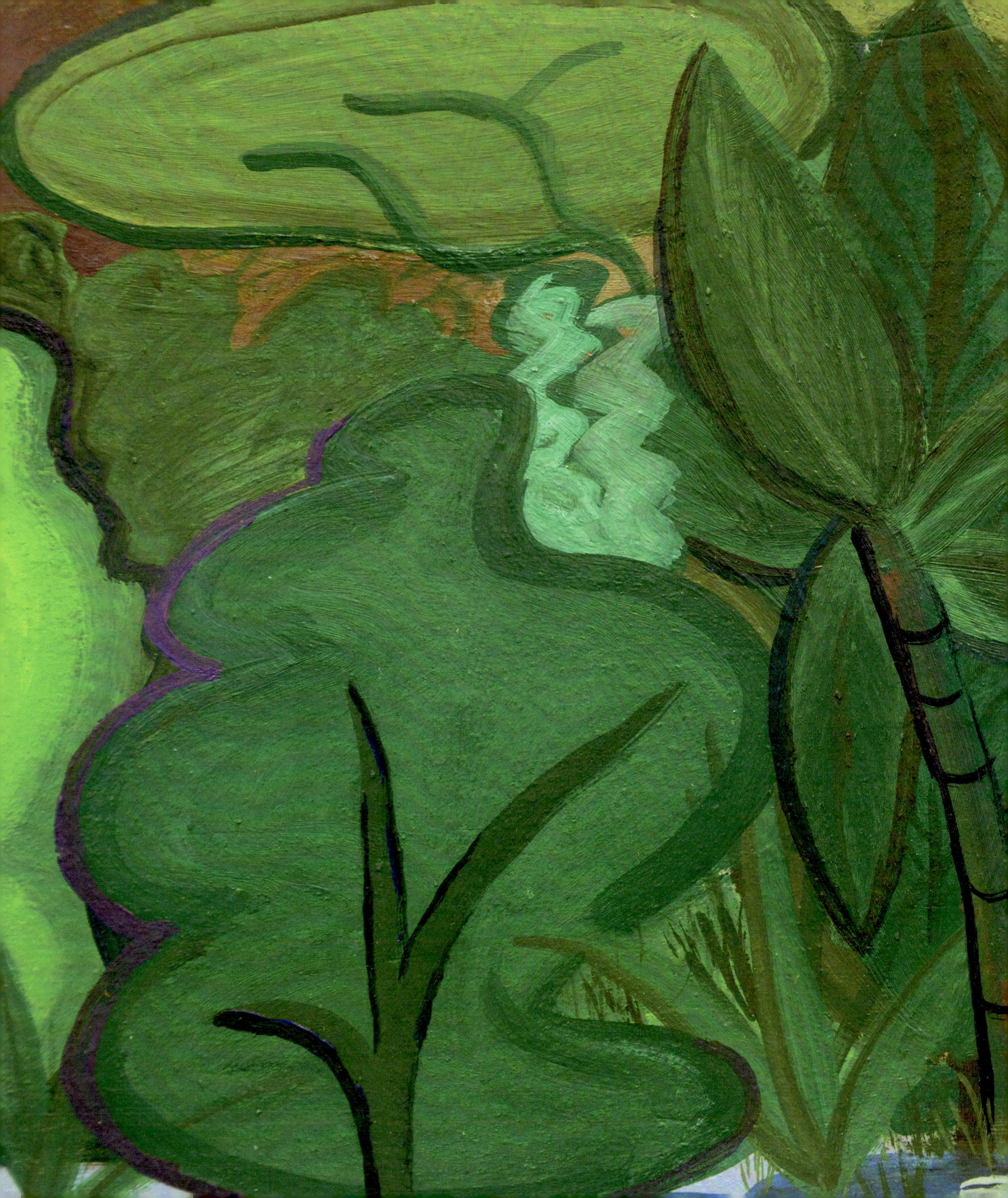

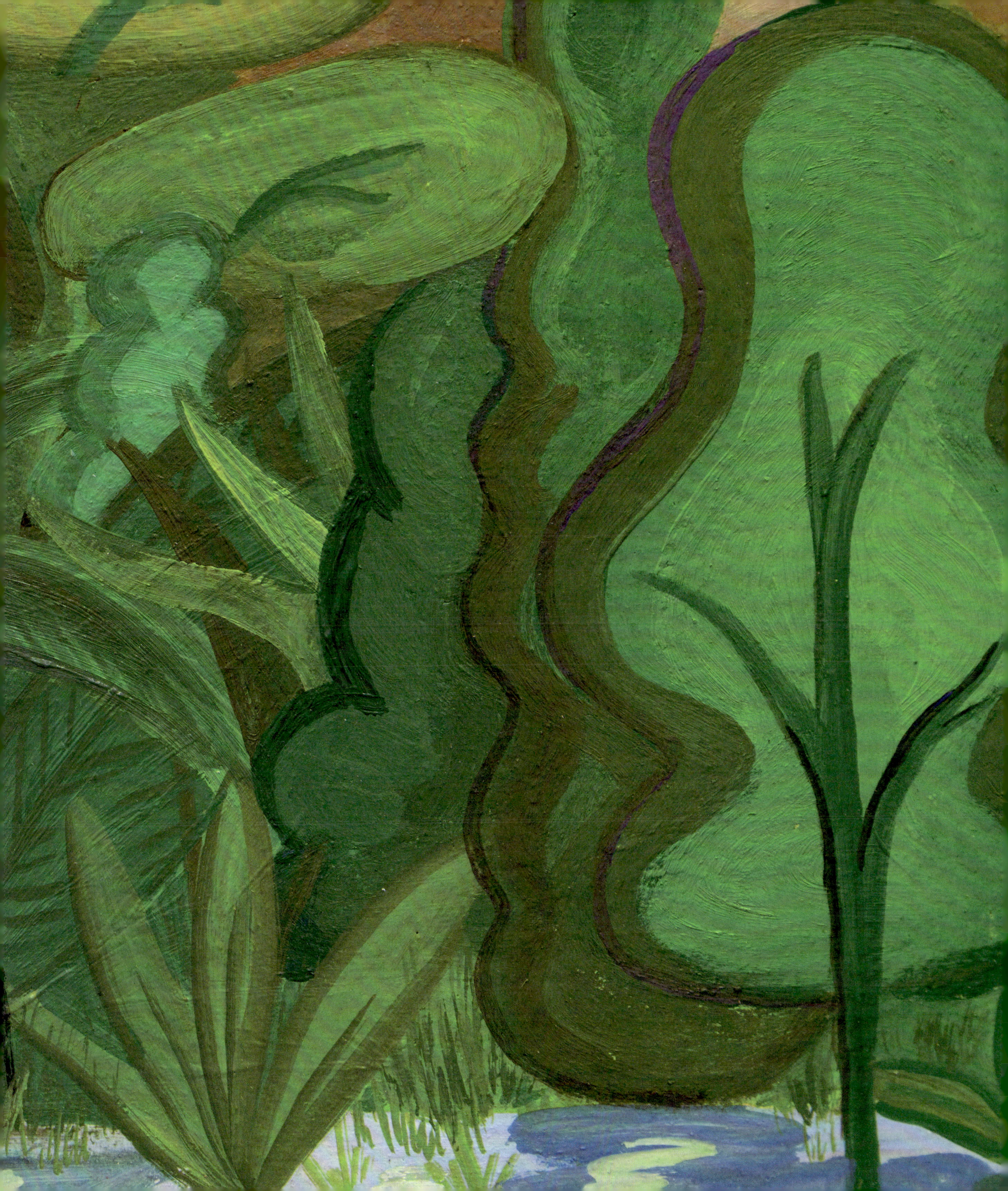

Morning light, 2022. Ceramic, glaze, wood, and lightbulb with wire,
48 × 20 × 20 in. (121.9 × 50.8 × 50.8 cm)

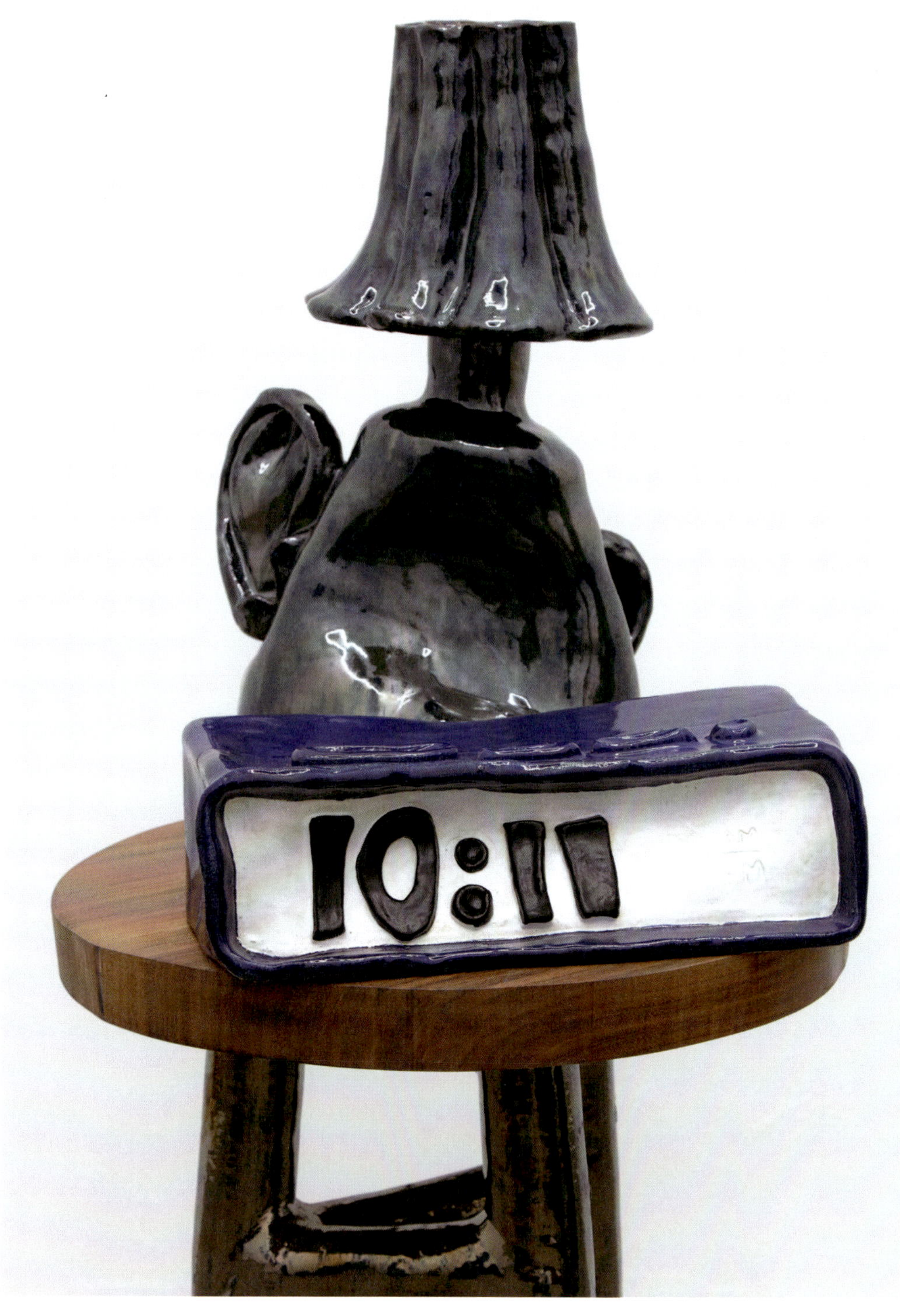

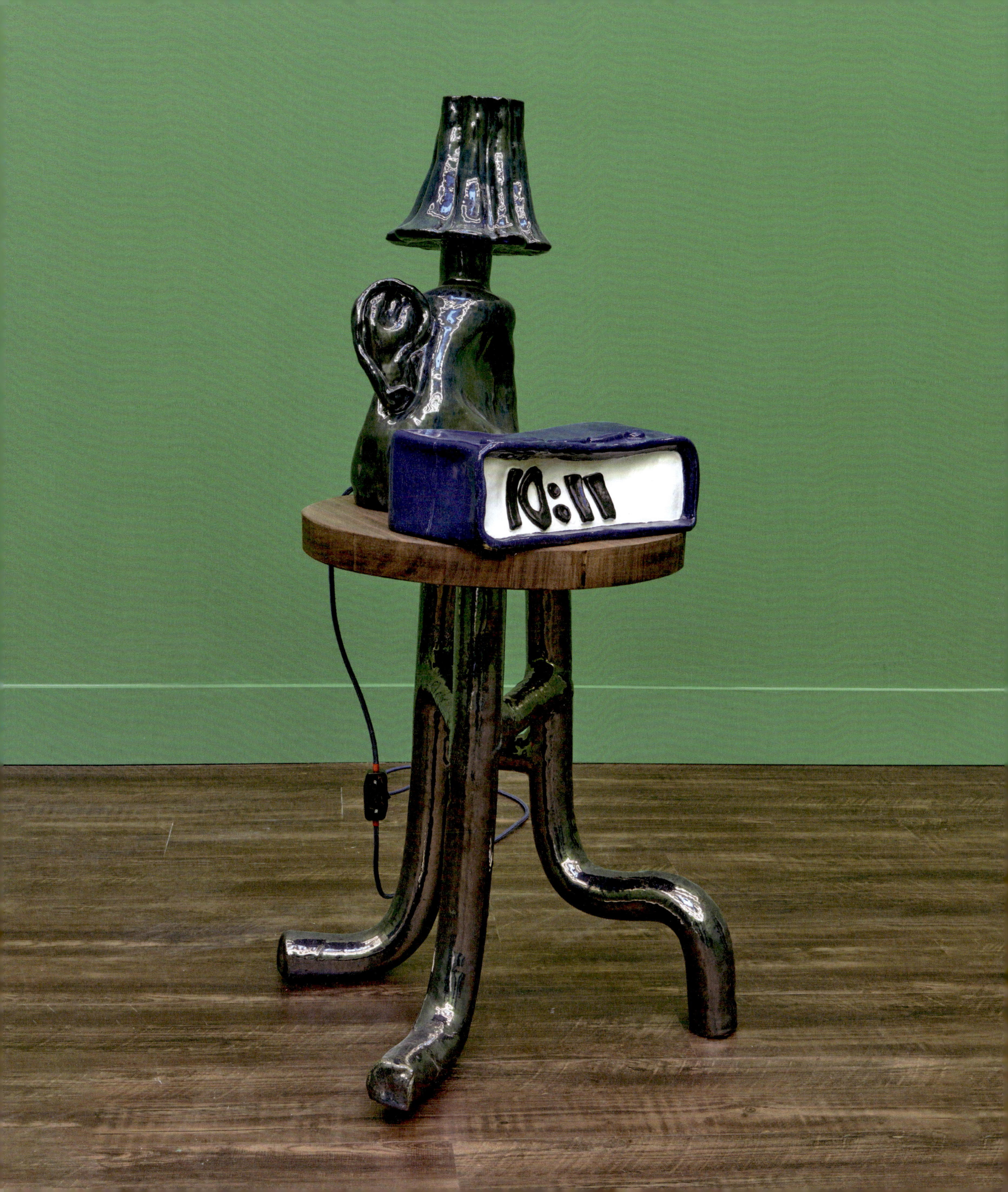
10:11

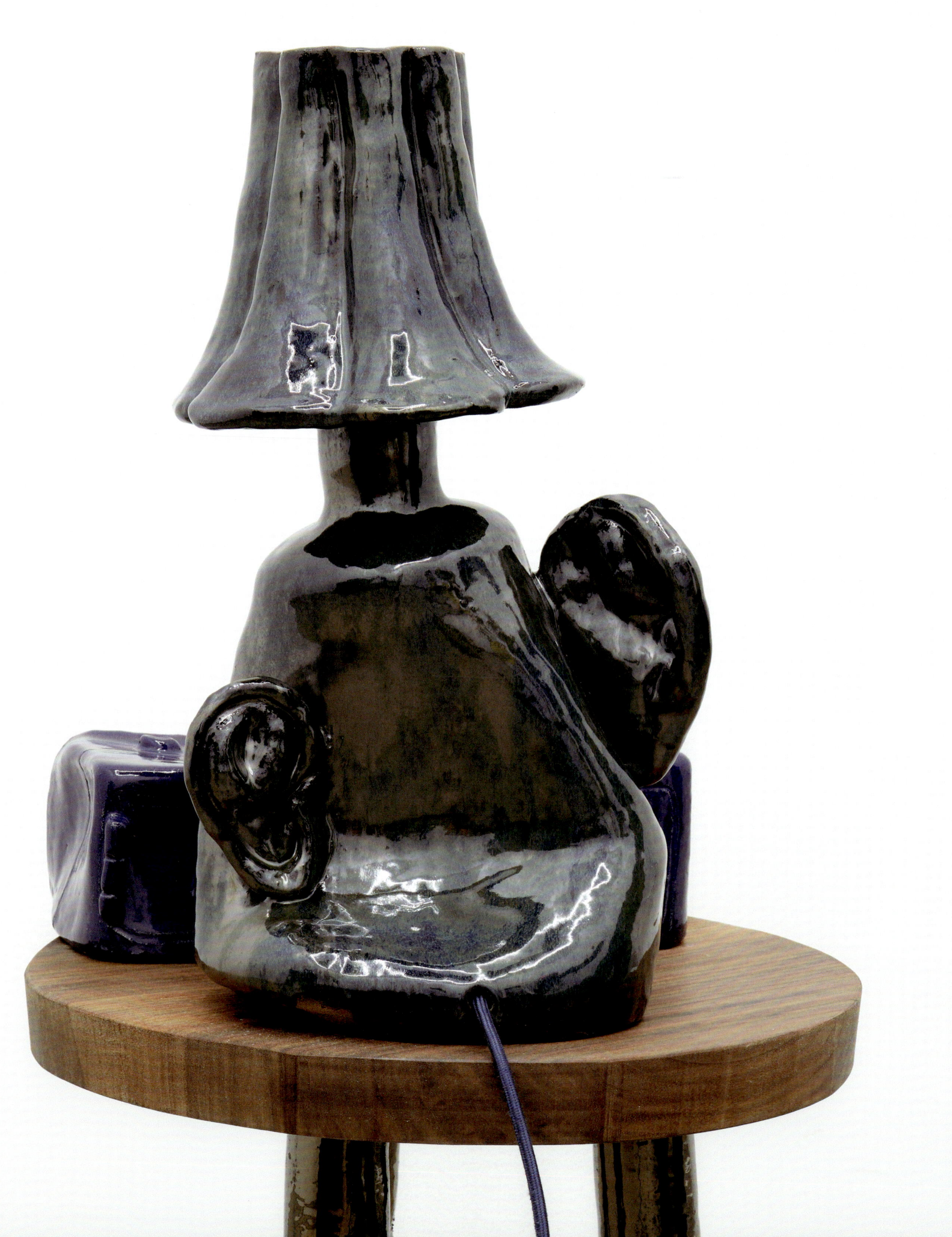

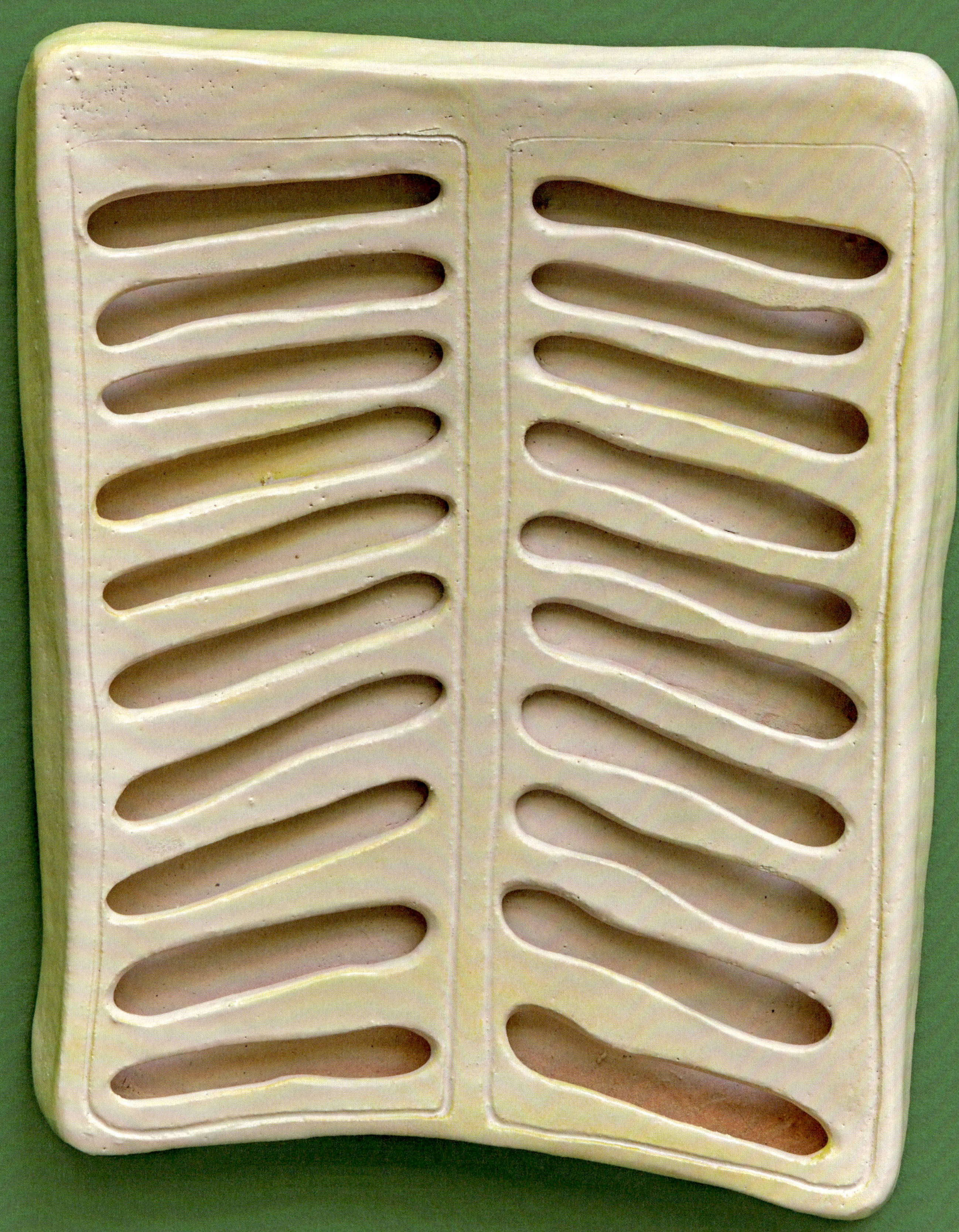

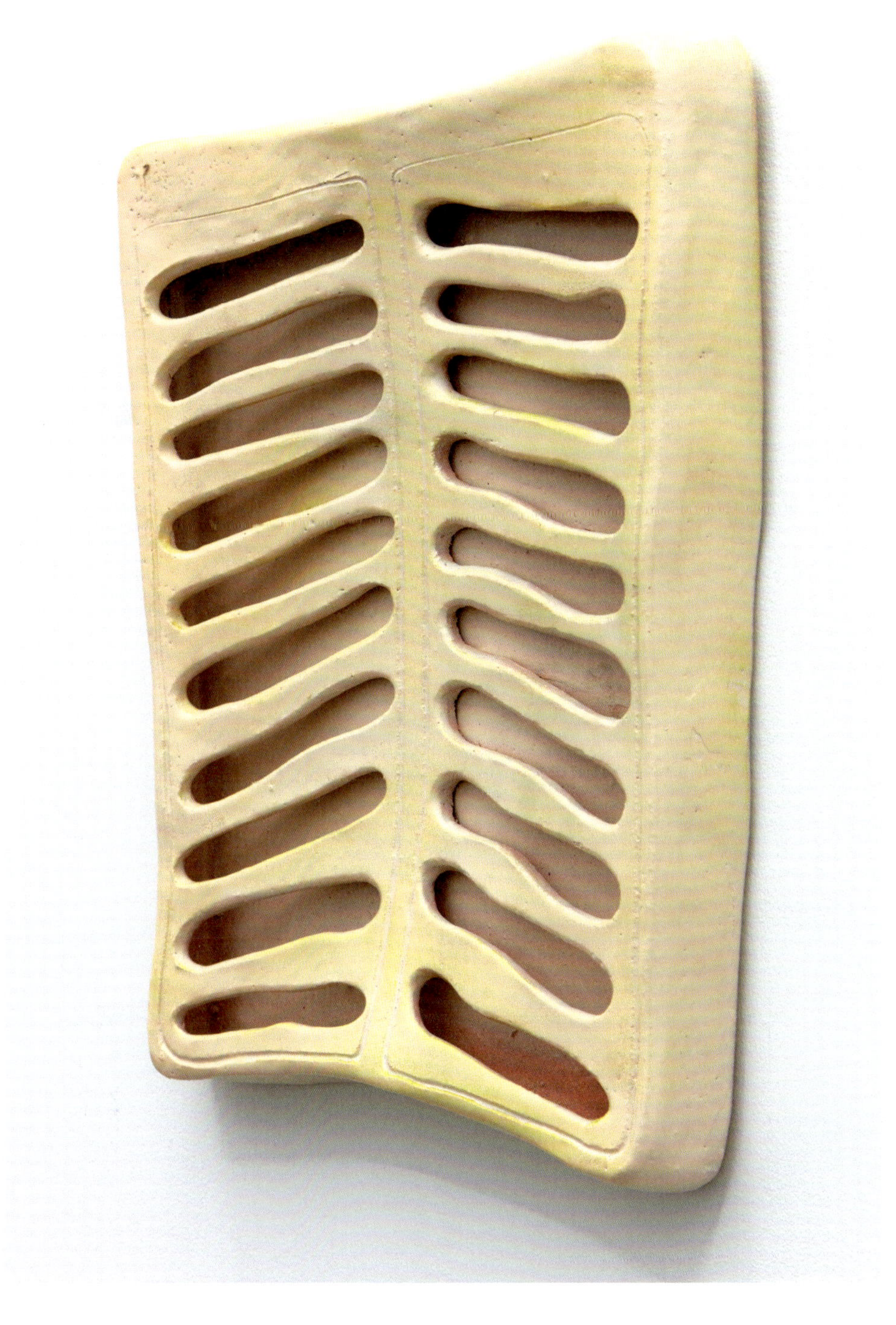

Bone broth, 2022. Ceramic and paint,
18 × 12 × 2 in. (45.7 × 30.5 × 5.1 cm)

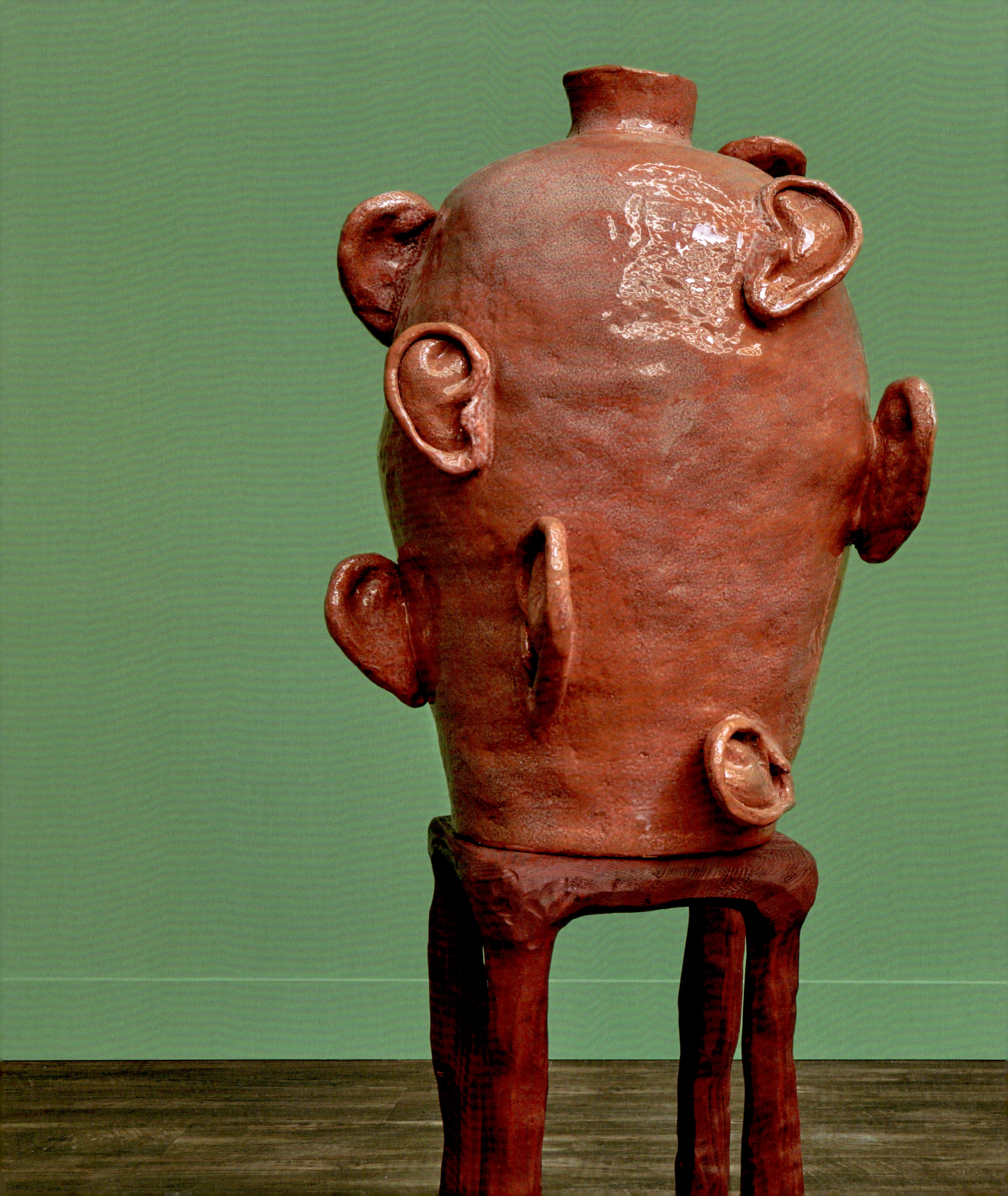

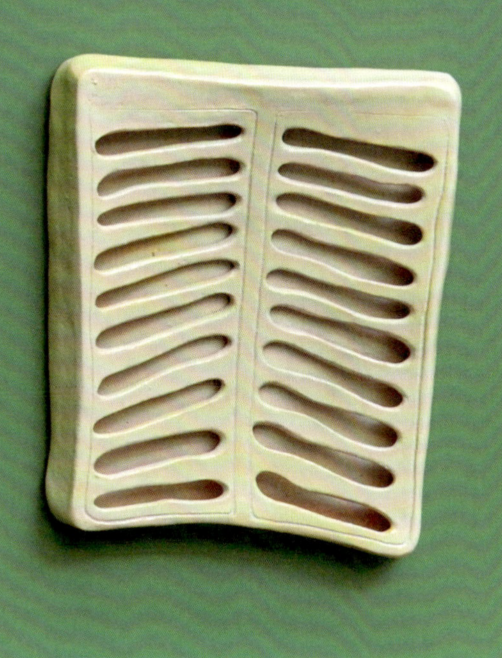

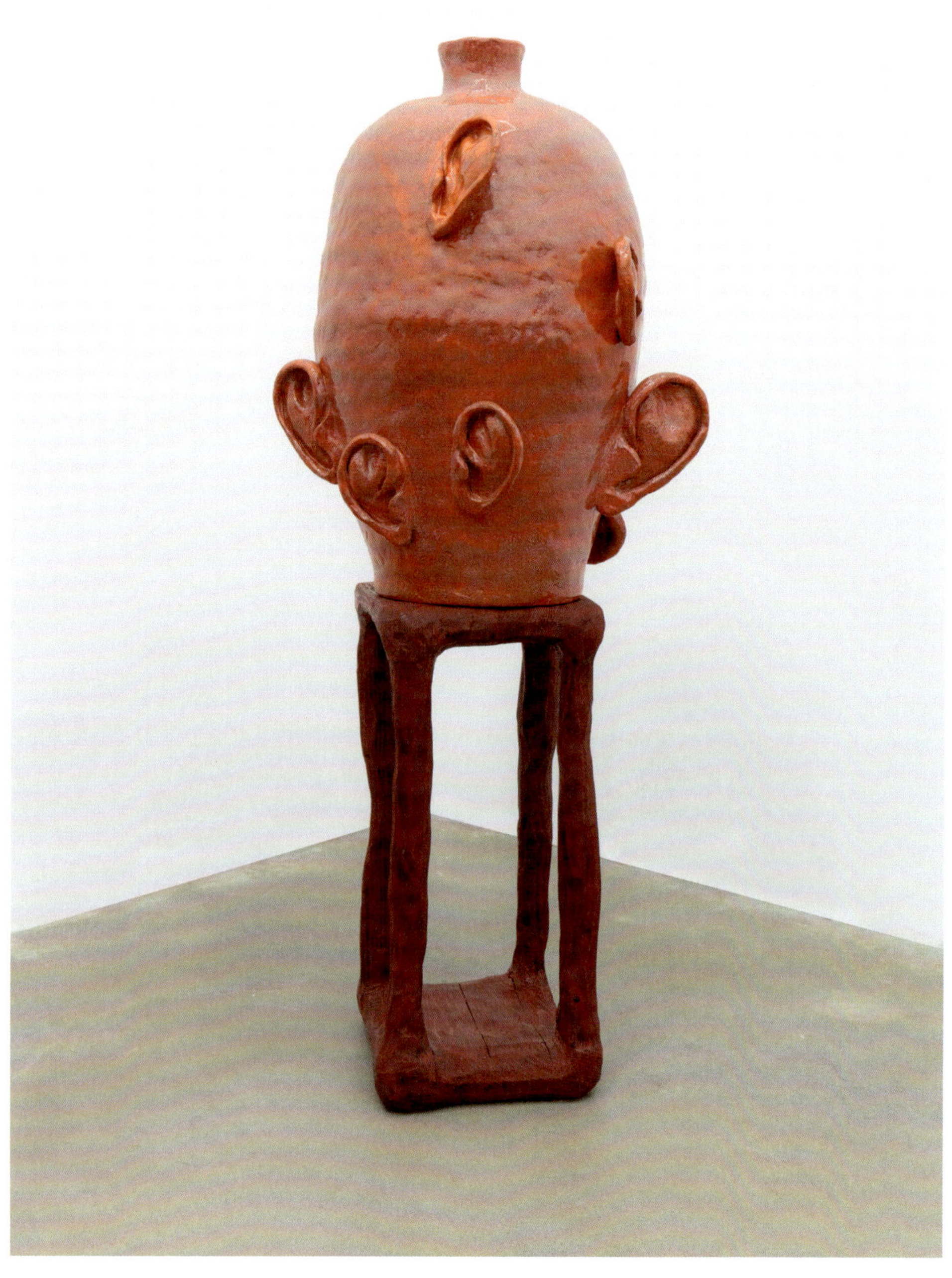

Secrets safe, 2022. Ceramic, glaze, and wood,
58½ × 22 × 22 in. (148.6 × 55.9 × 55.9 cm)

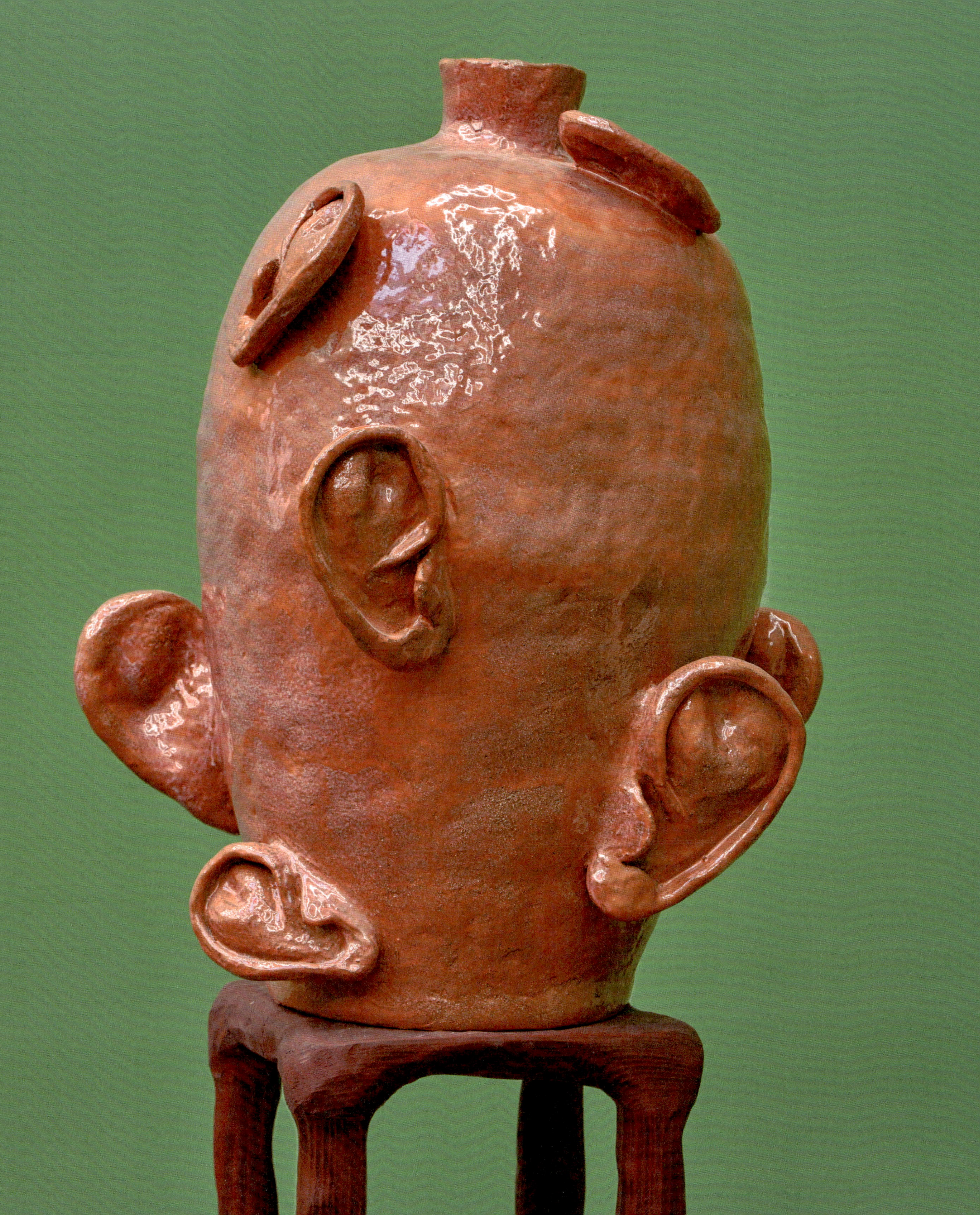

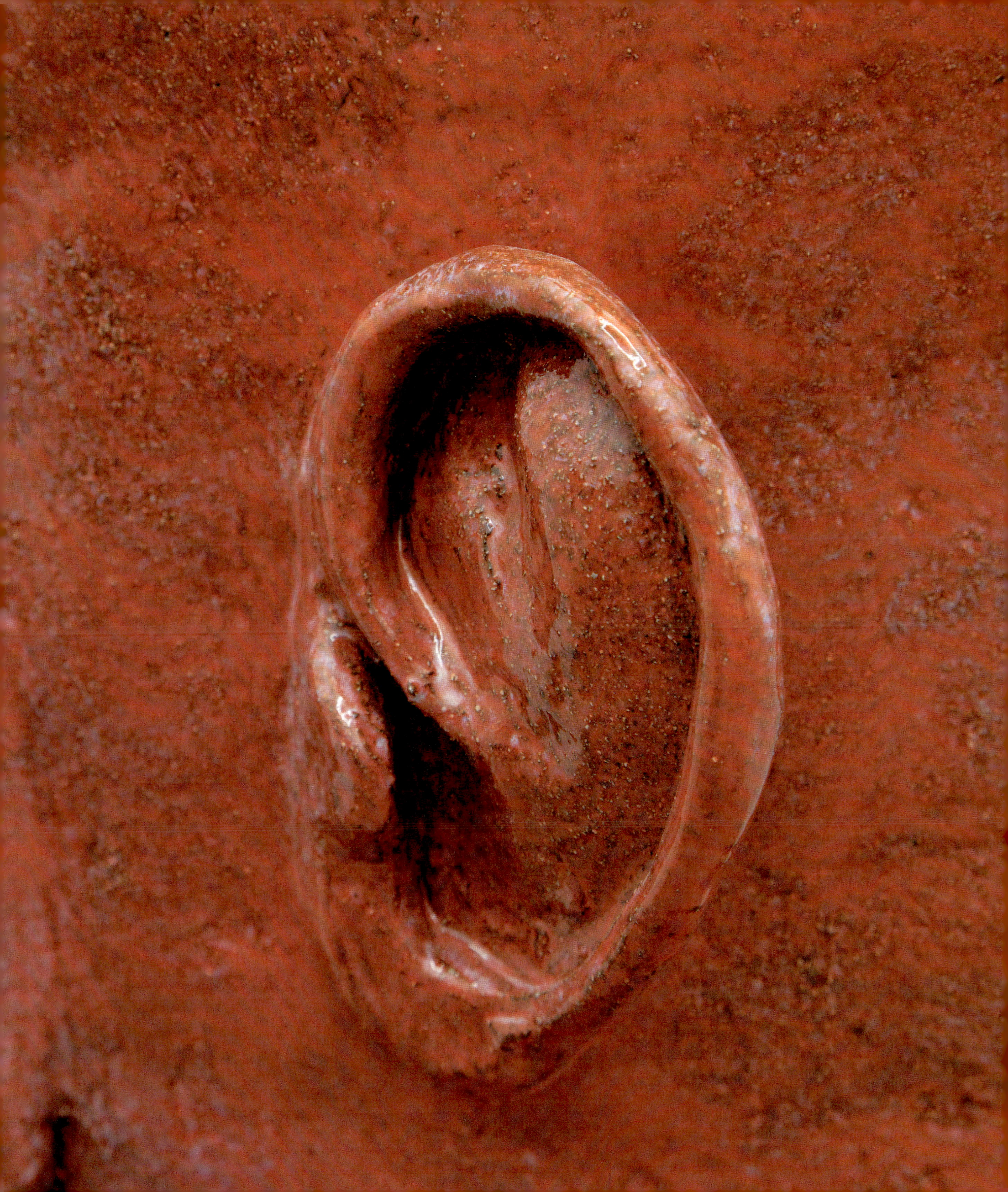

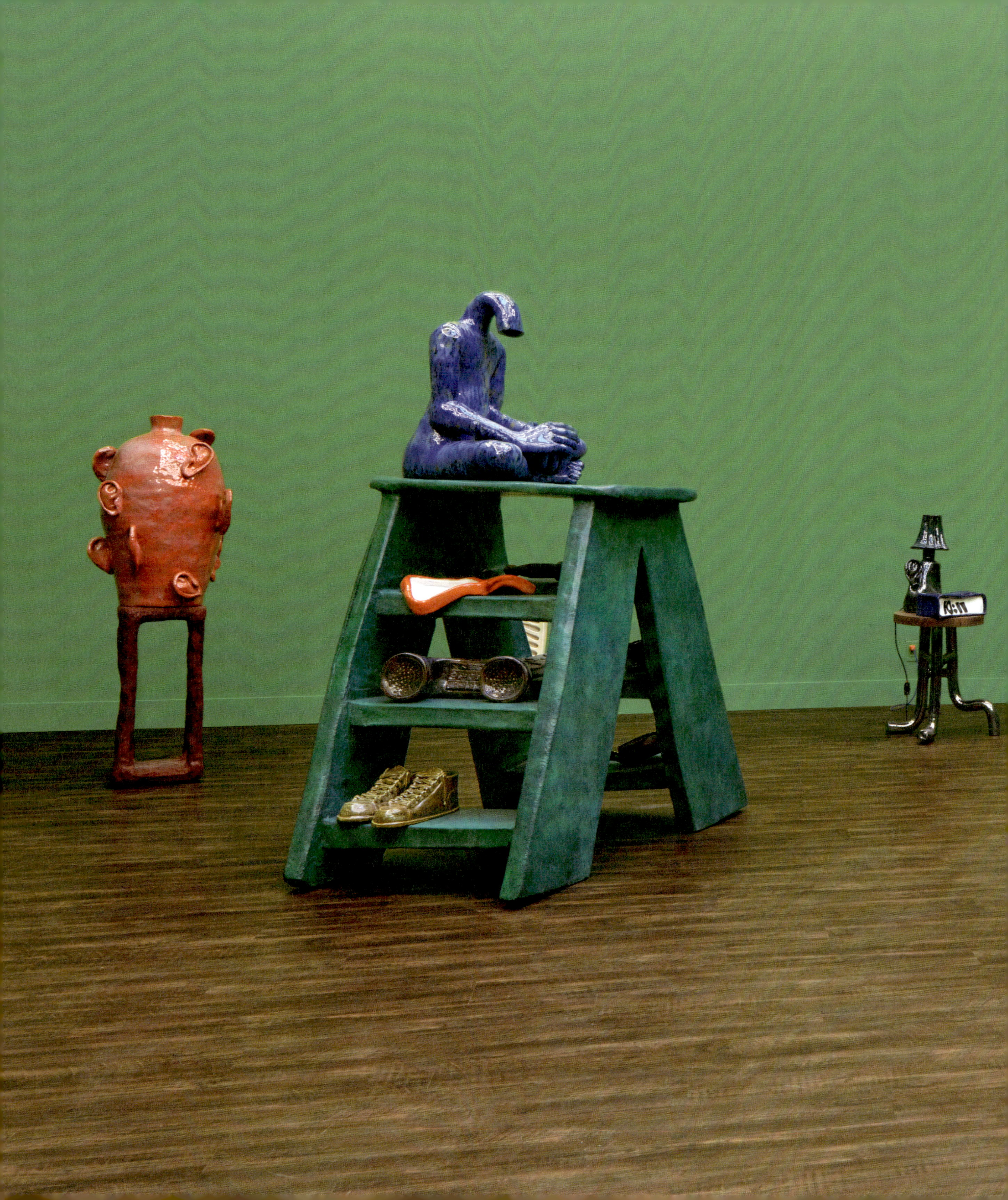

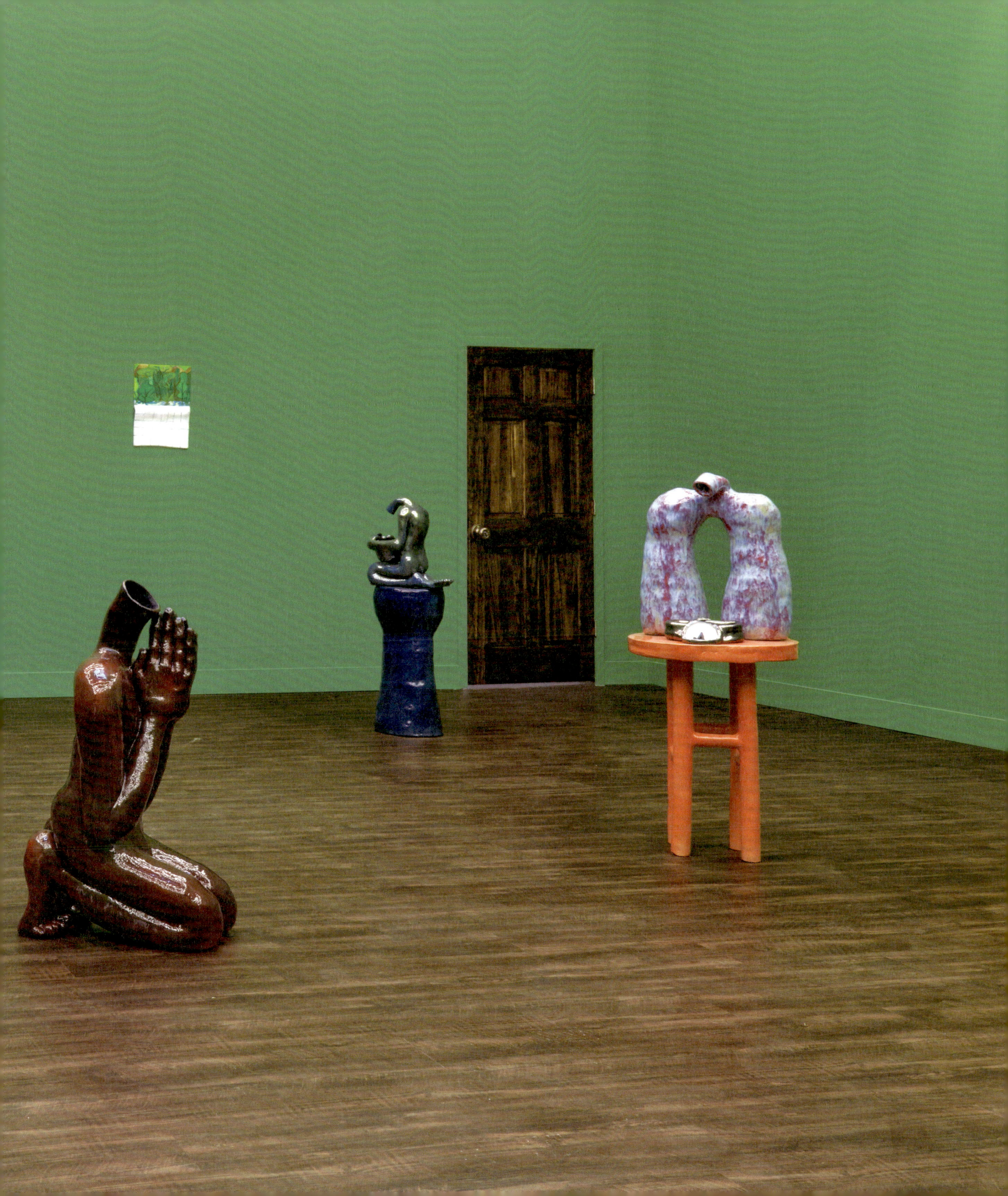

Tools, 2022. Bronze with glazed ceramics,
48 × 32½ × 61 in. (121.9 × 82.6 × 154.9 cm)

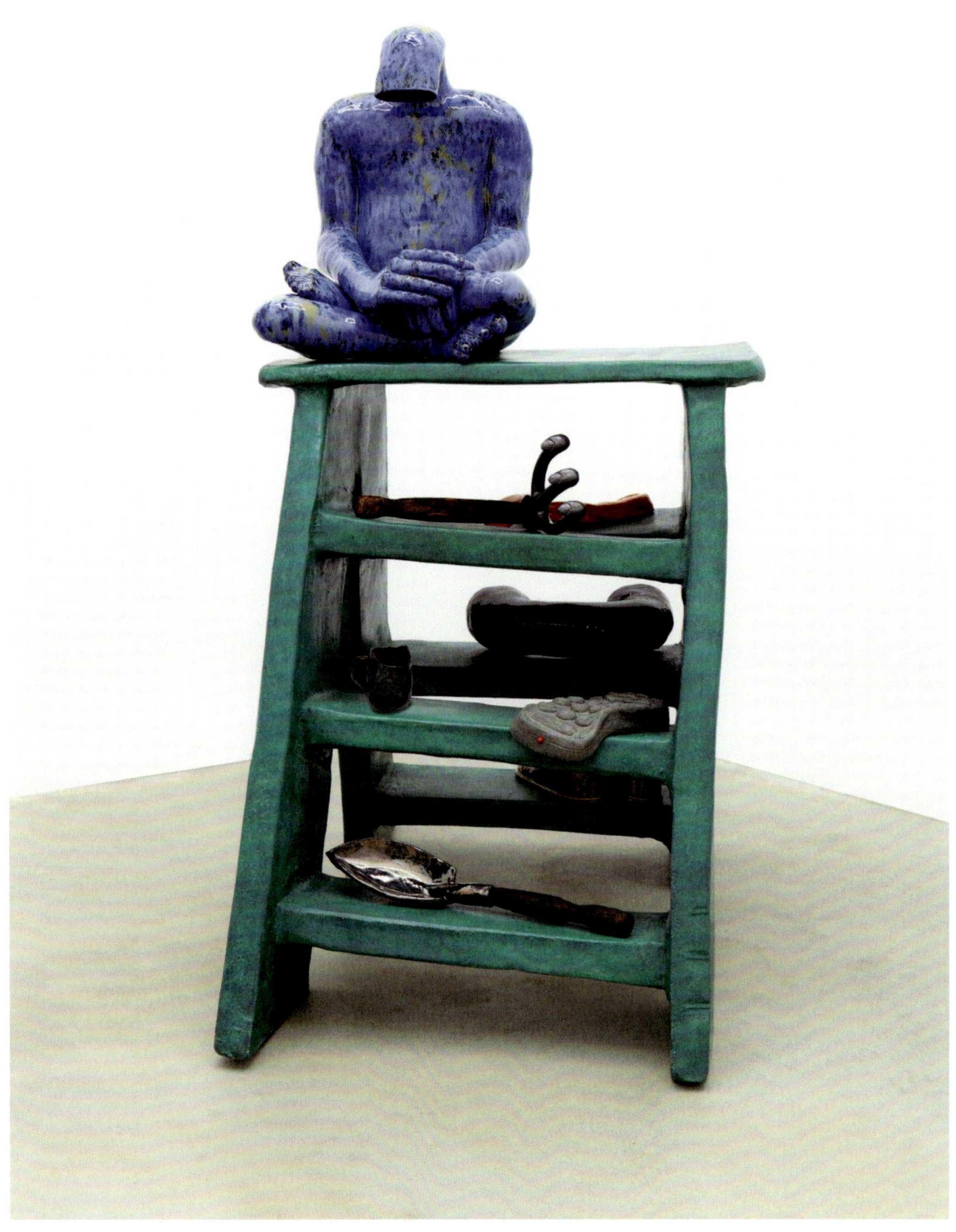

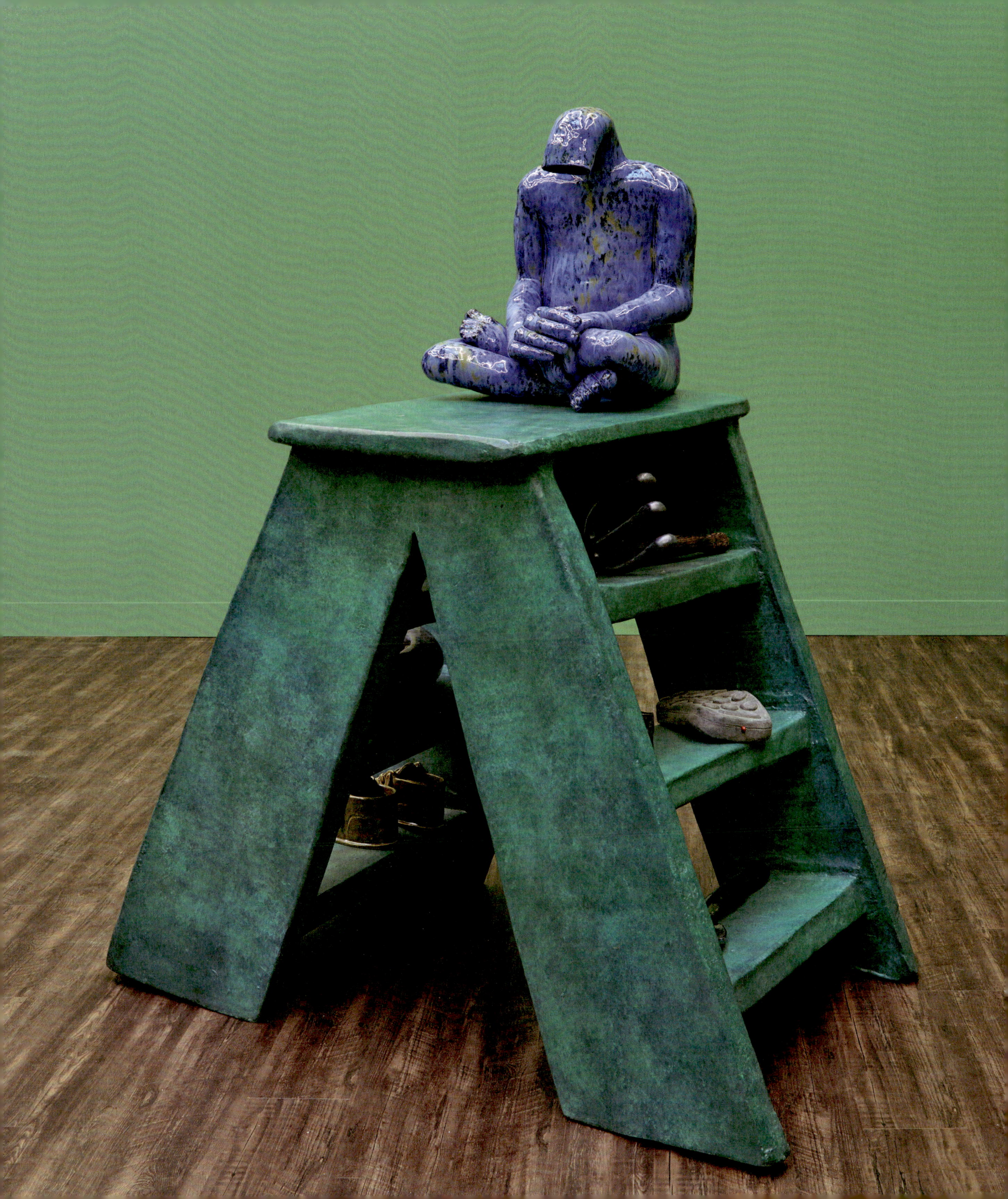

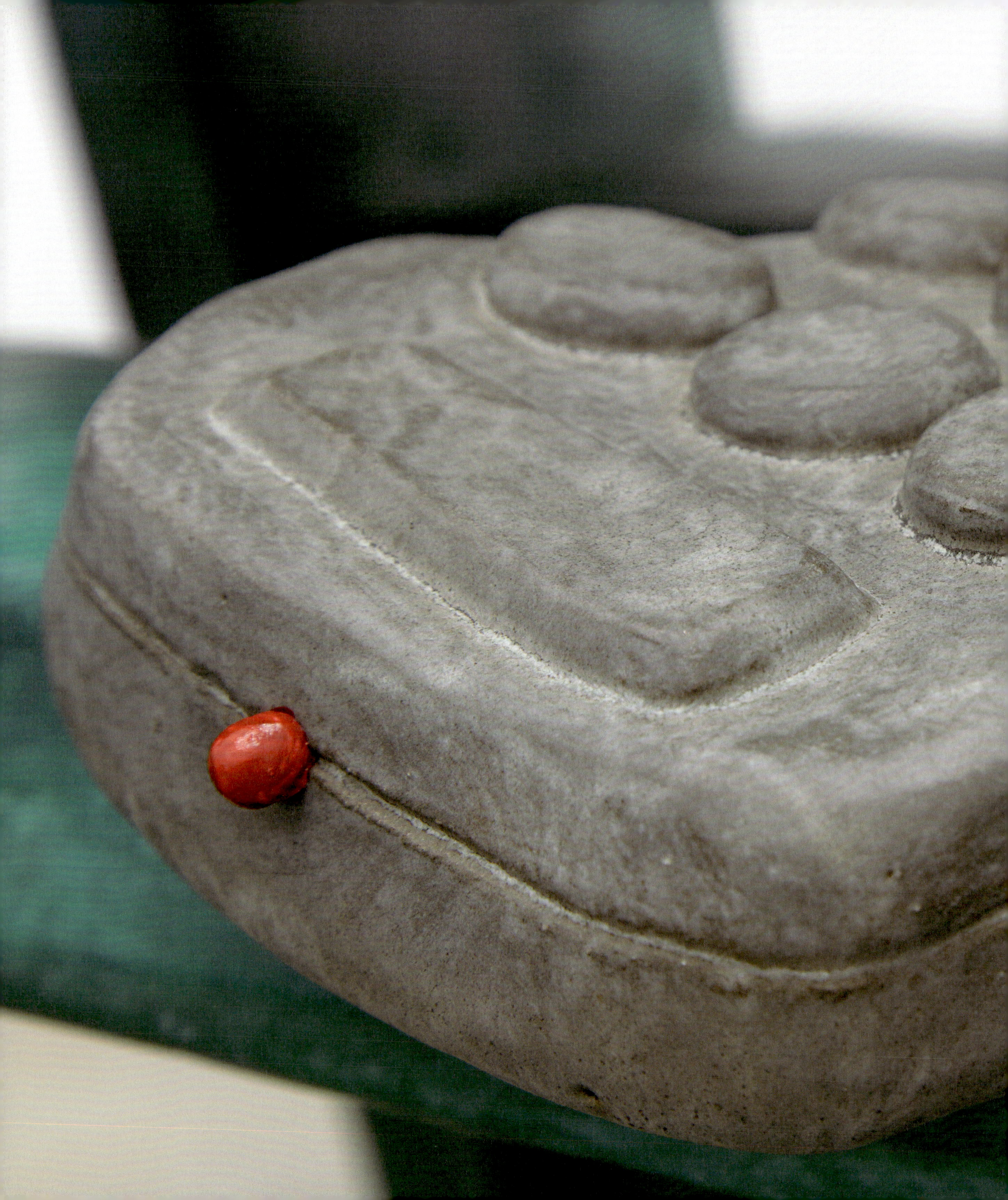

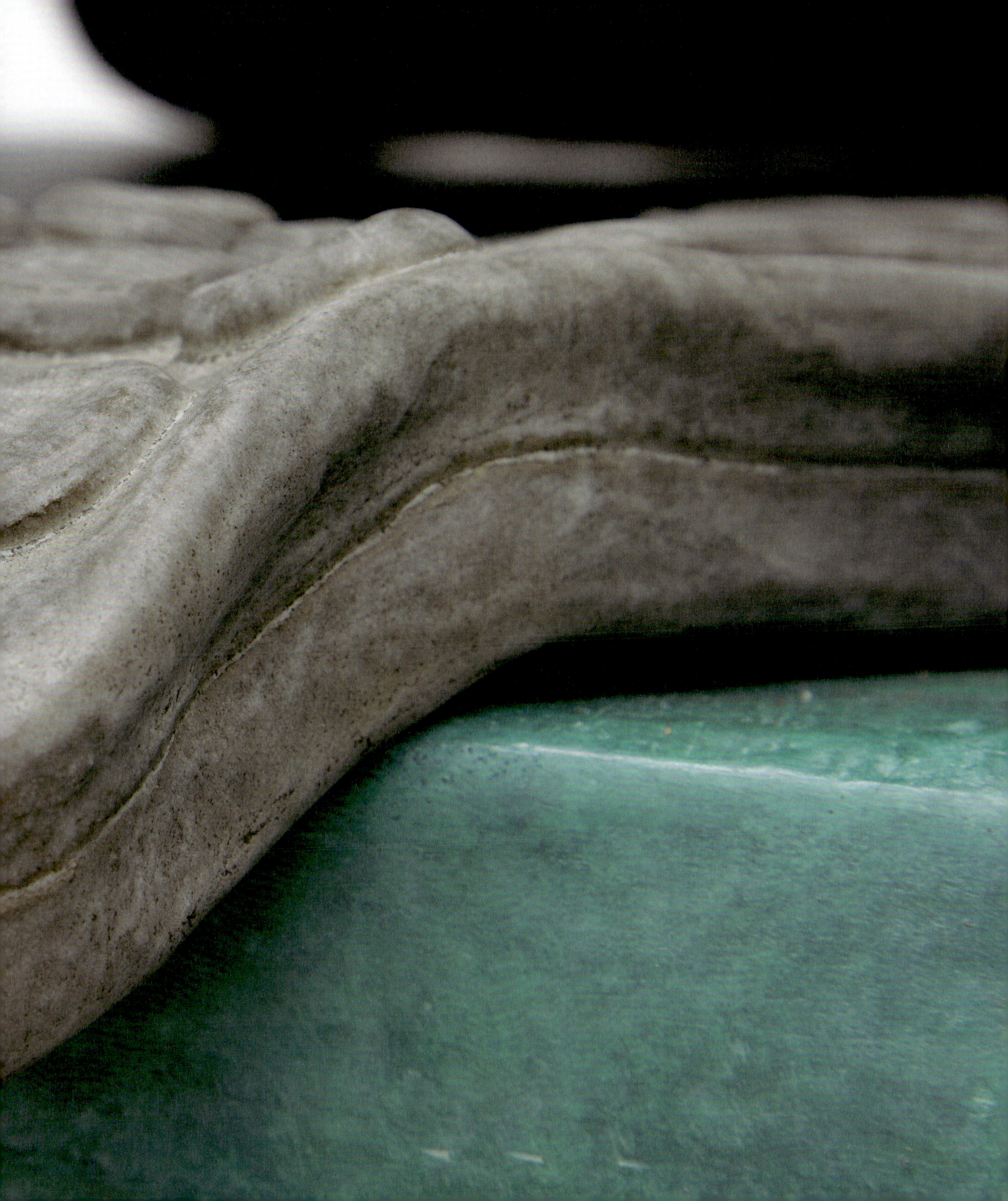

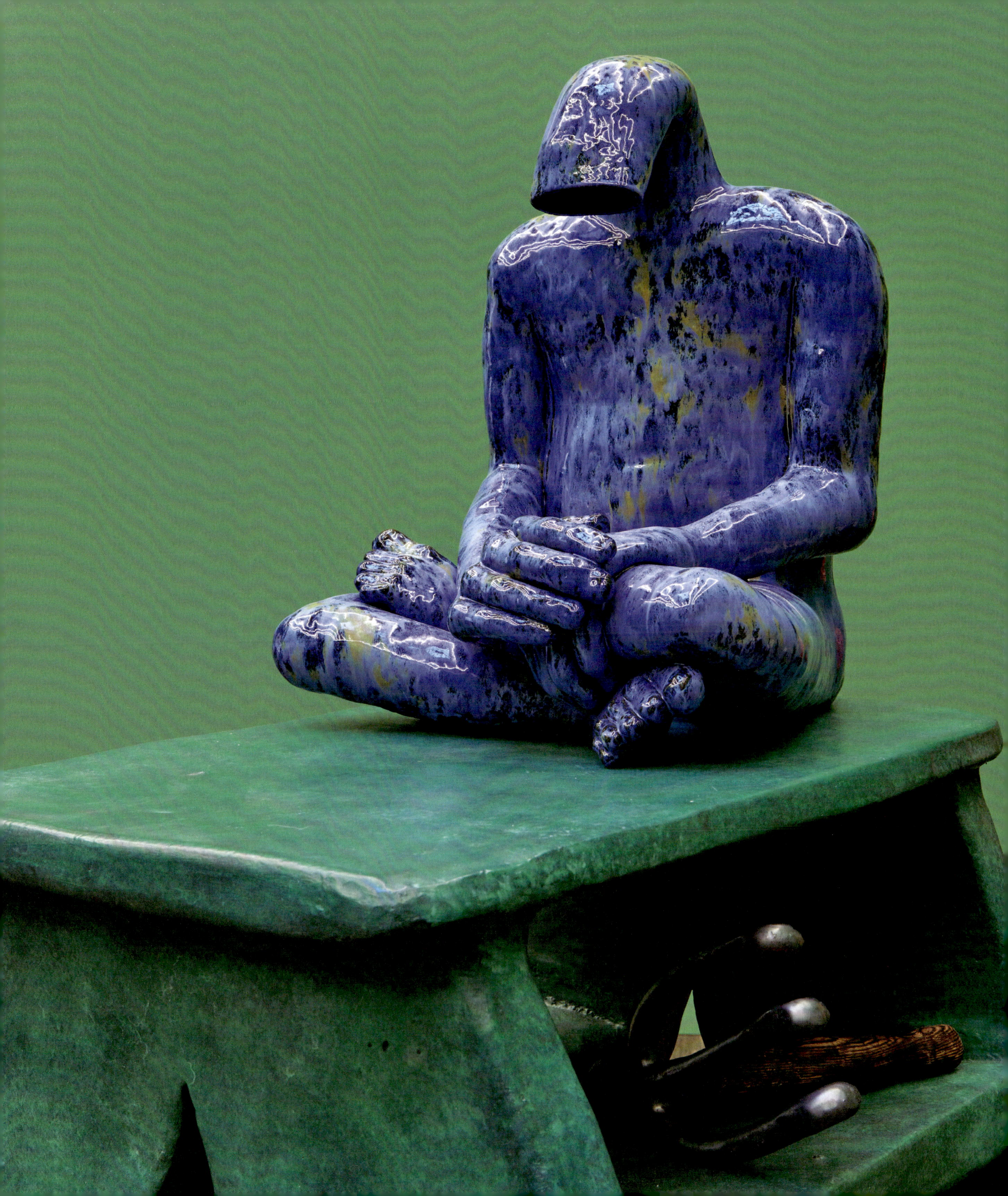

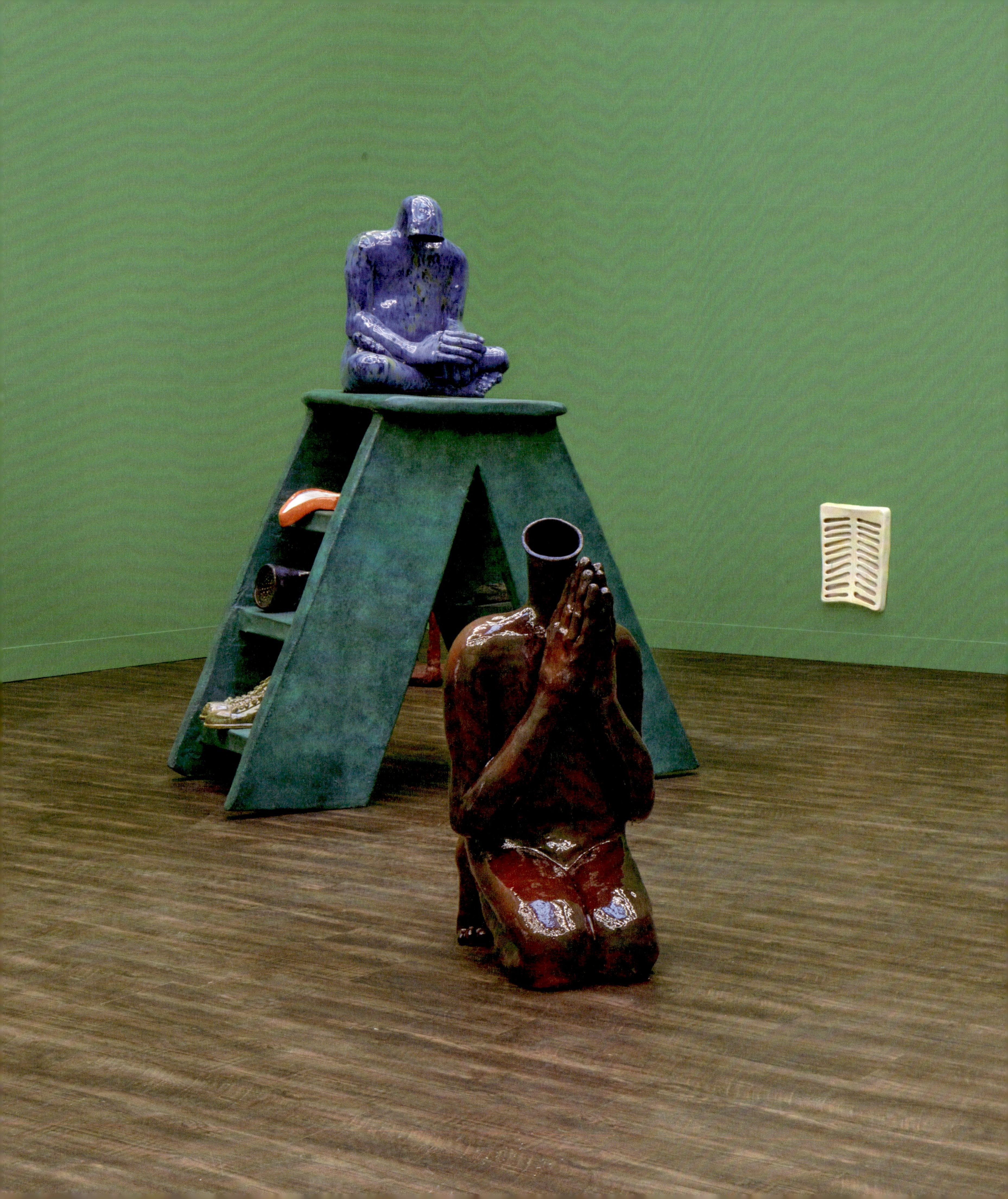

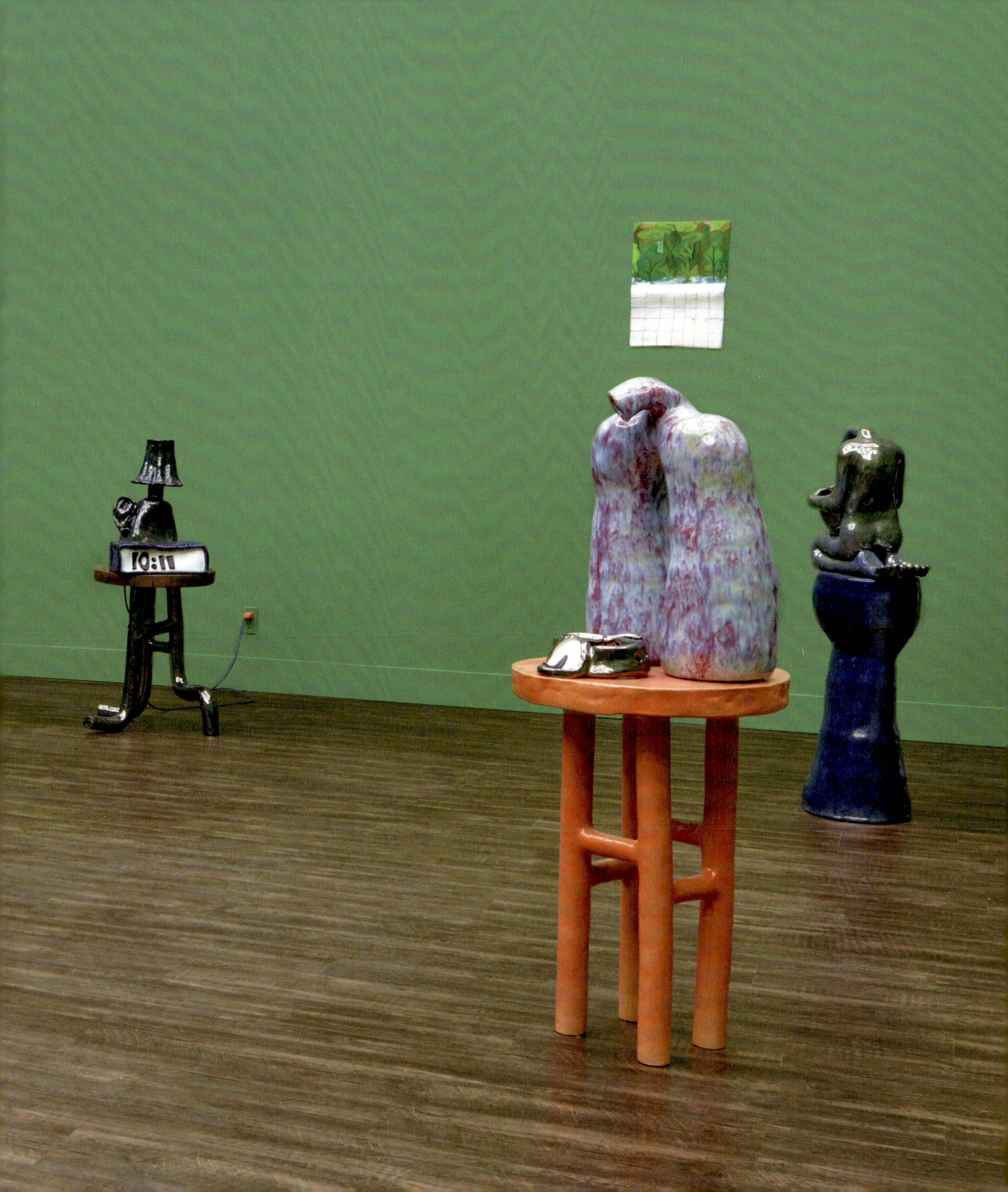

On my way home, 2022. Ceramic, paint, and resin,
40 × 20 × 22 in. (101.6 × 50.8 × 55.9 cm)

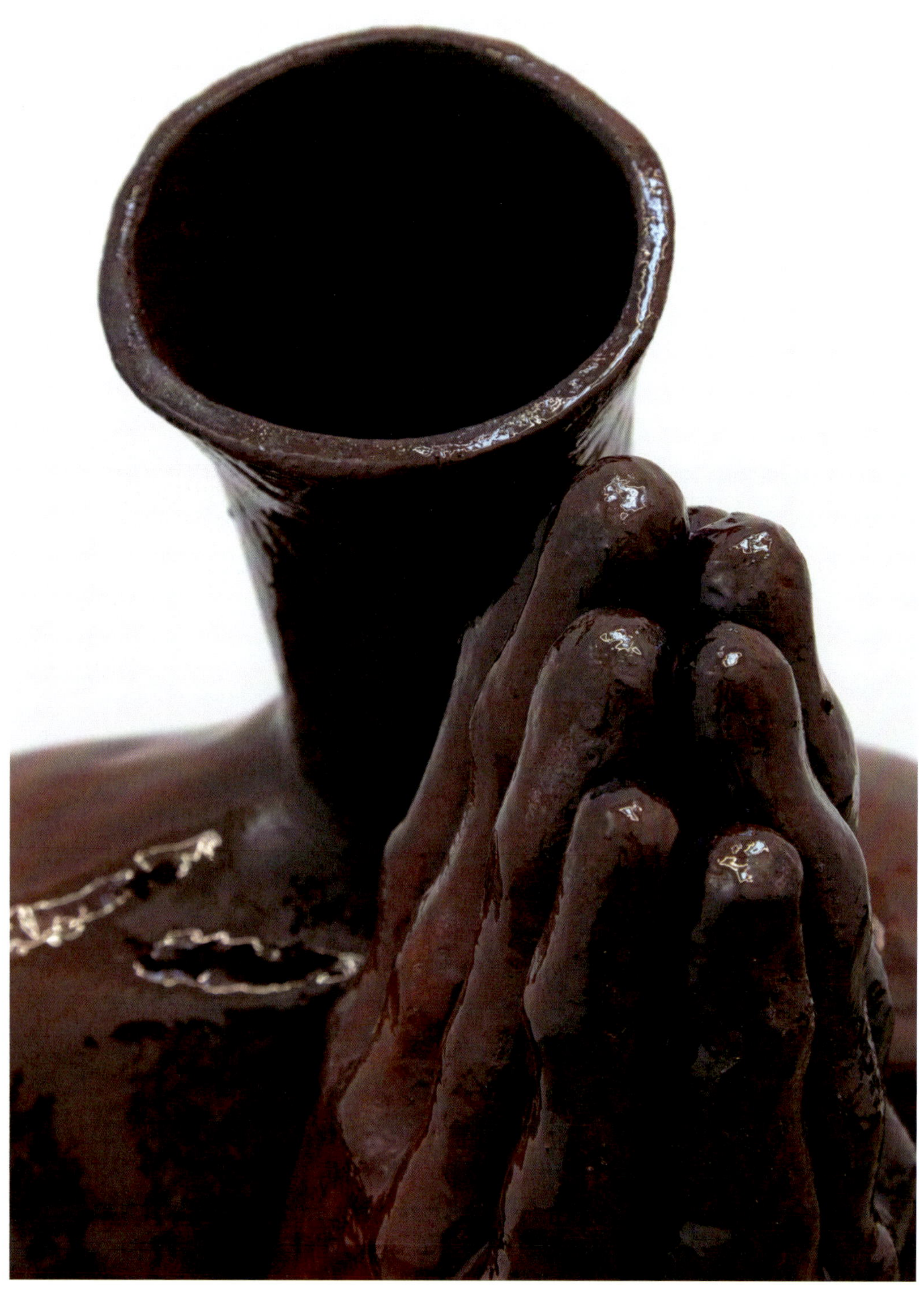

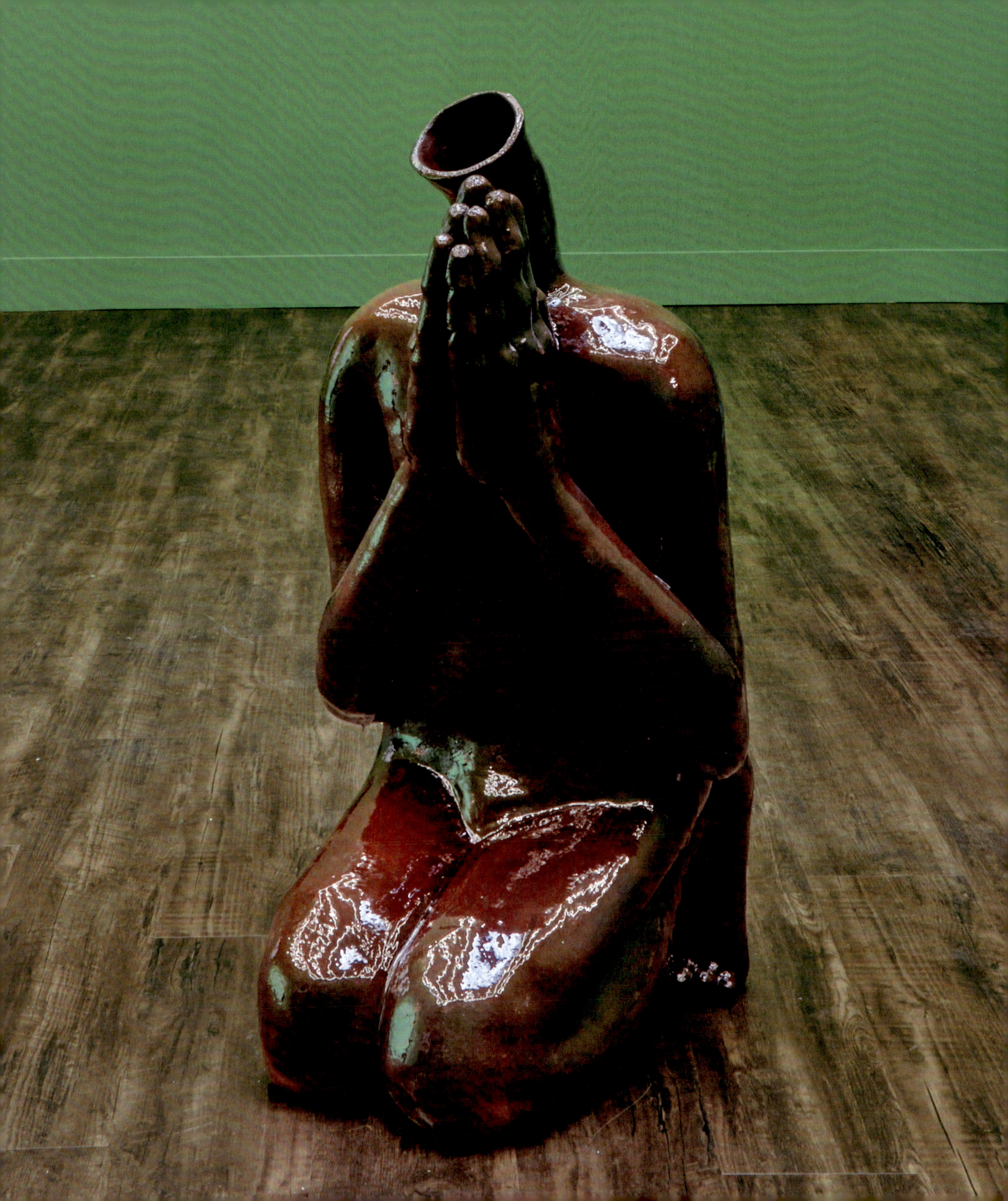

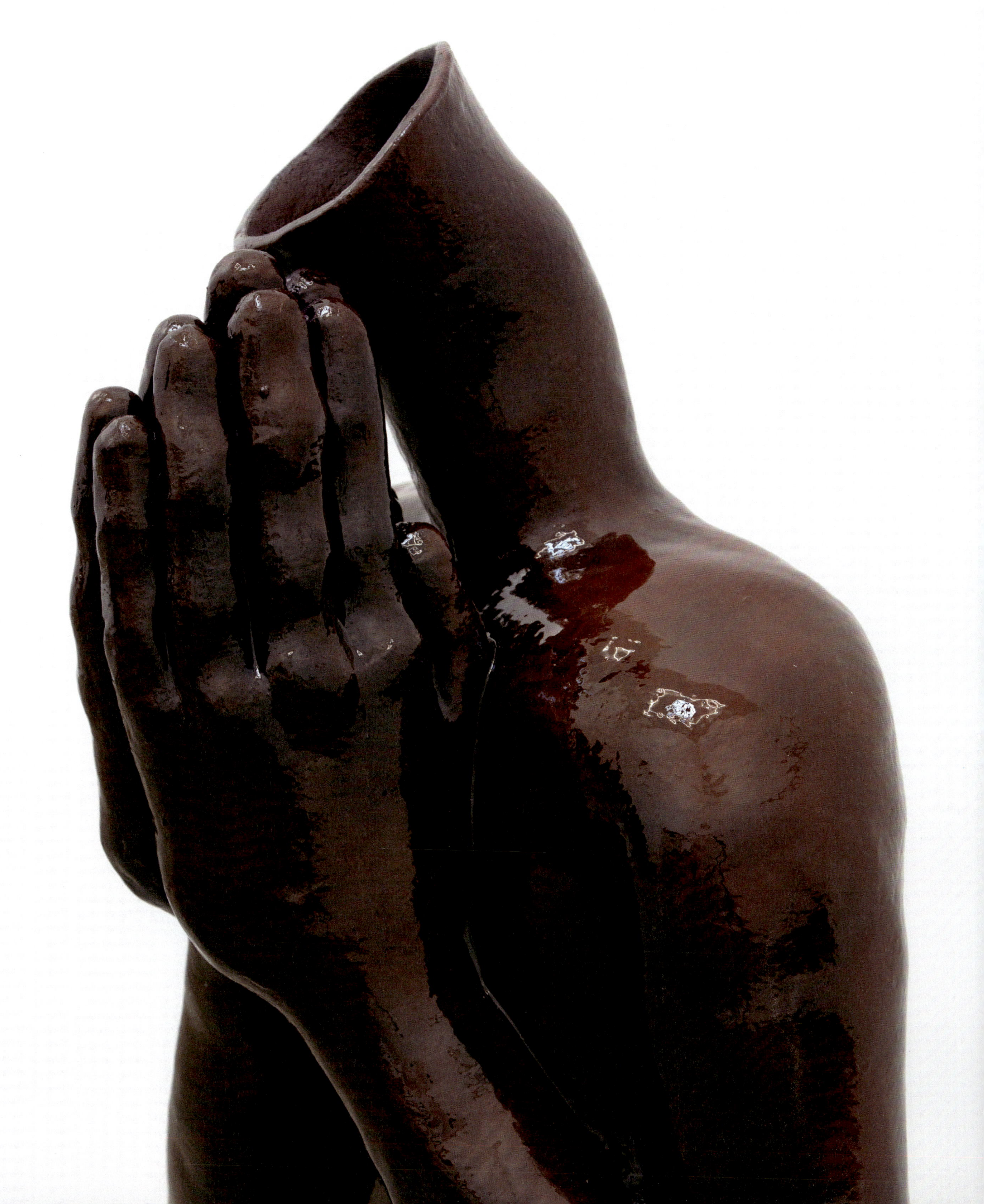

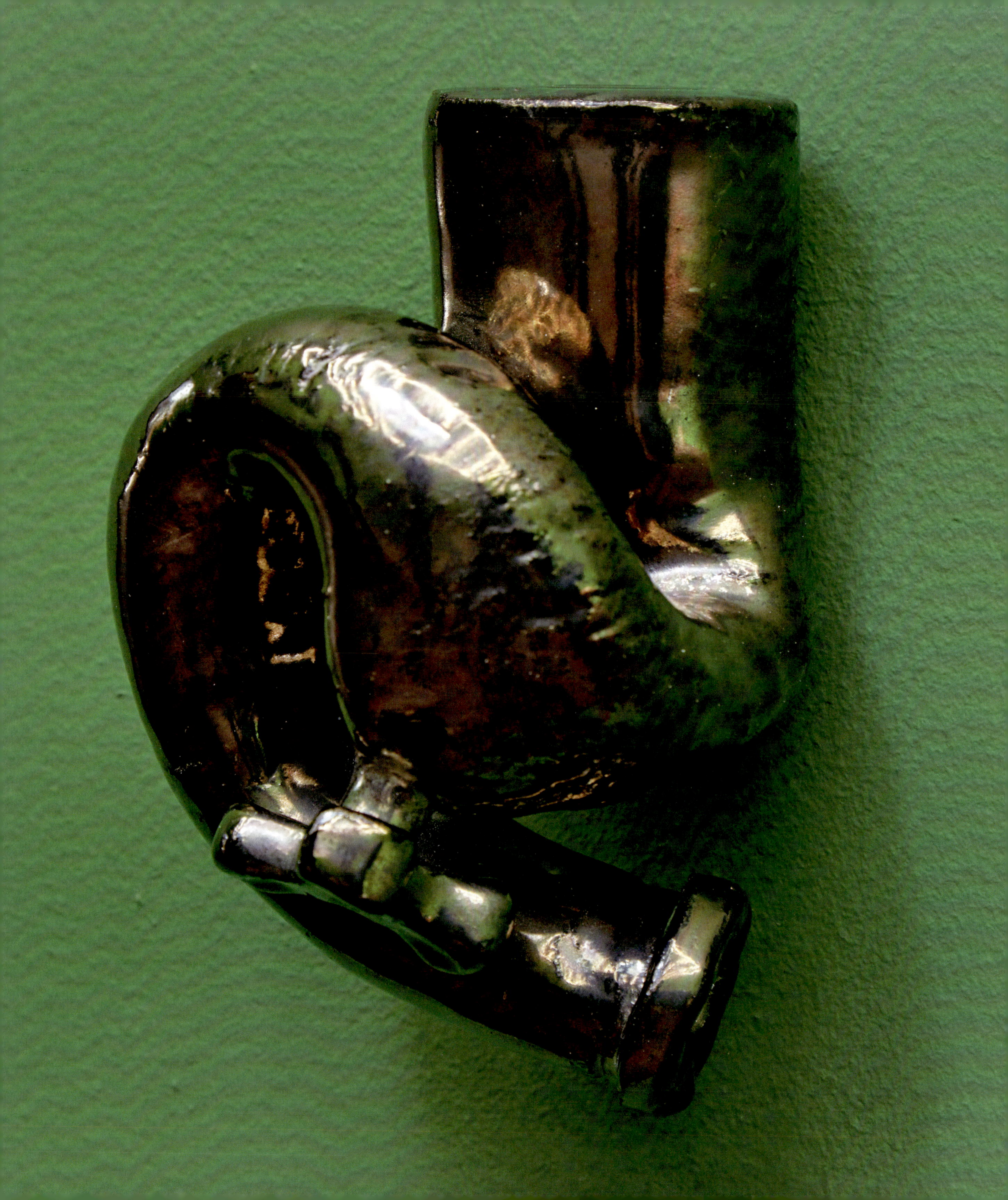

Faucet, 2022. Ceramic and glaze,
8 × 6 × 6 in. (20.3 × 15.2 × 15.2 cm)

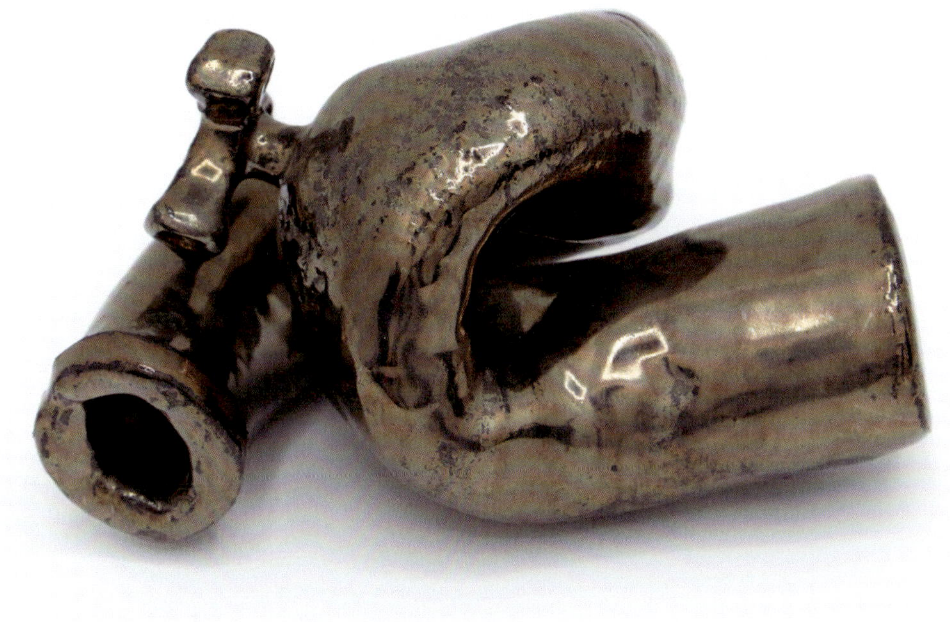

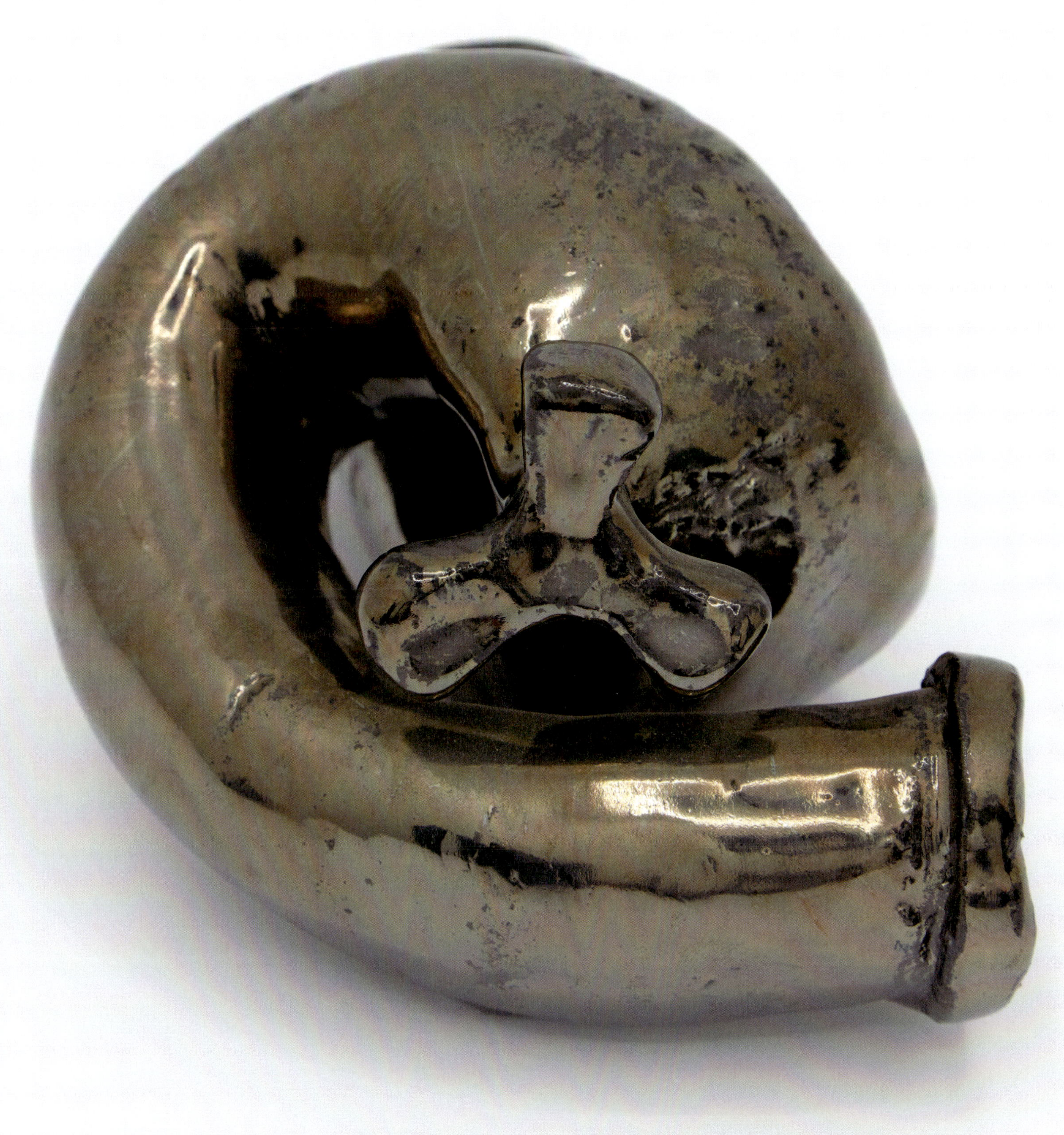

Every last drop, 2022. Ceramic and glaze,
47 × 21 × 21 in. (119.4 × 53.3 × 53.3 cm)

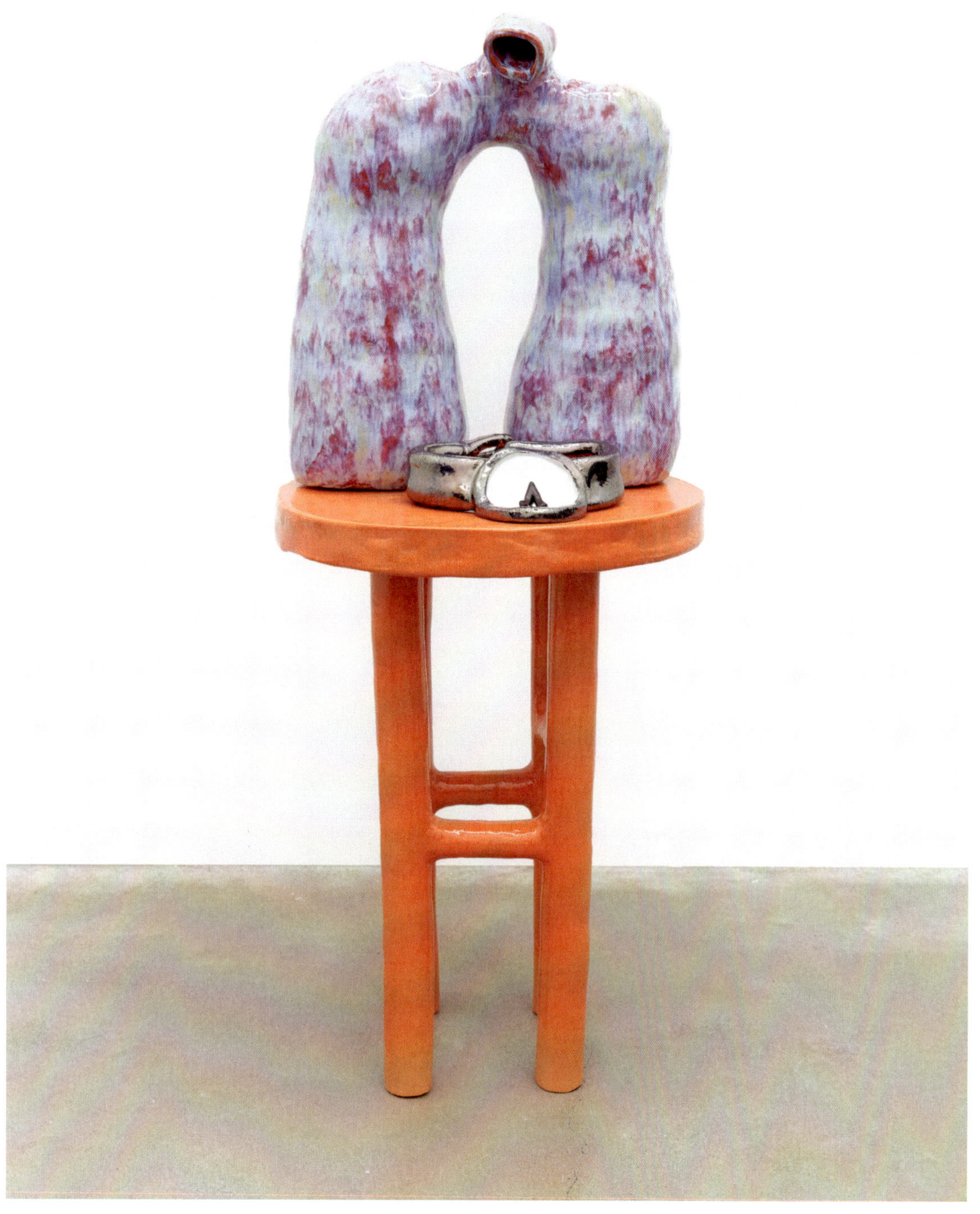

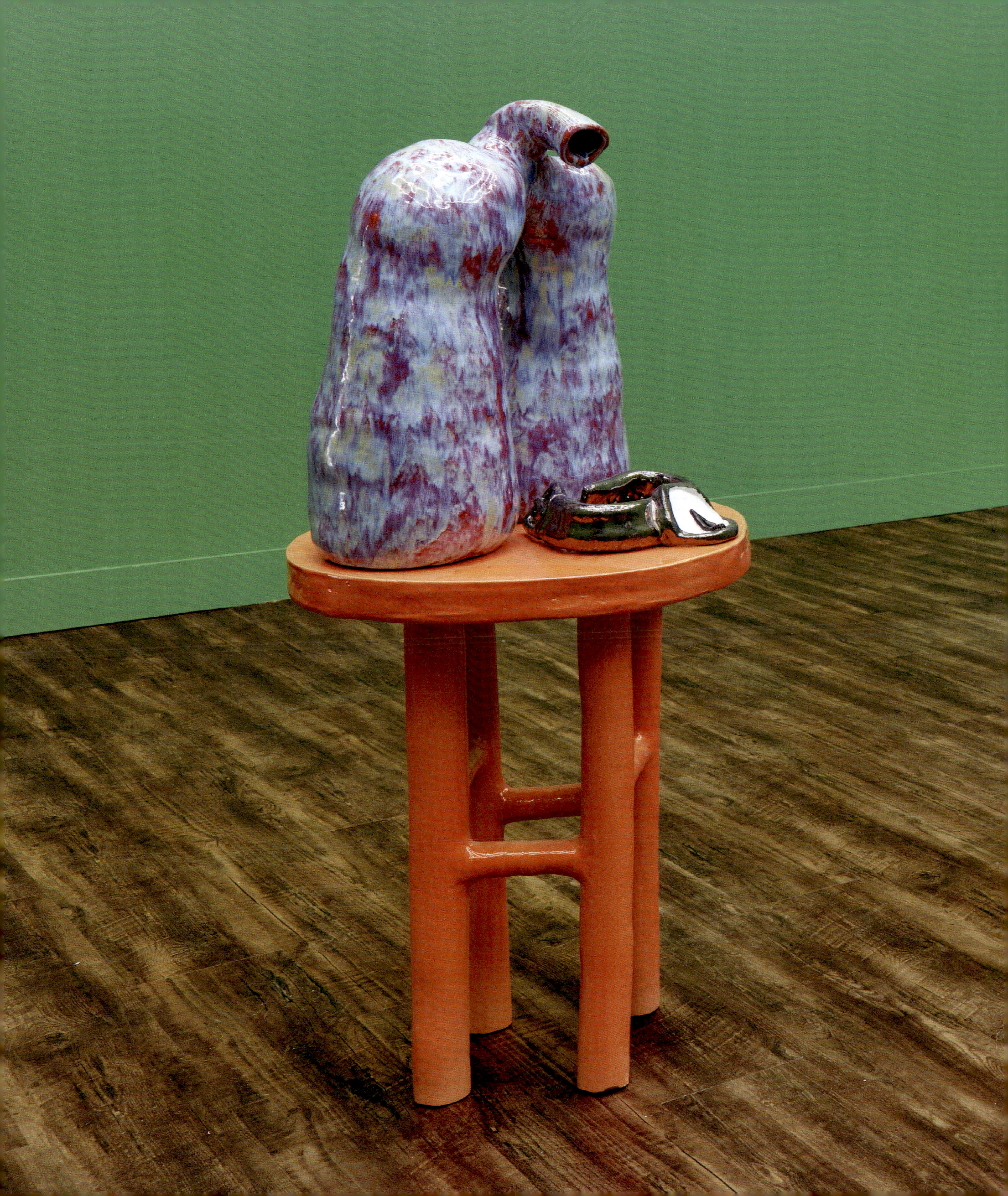

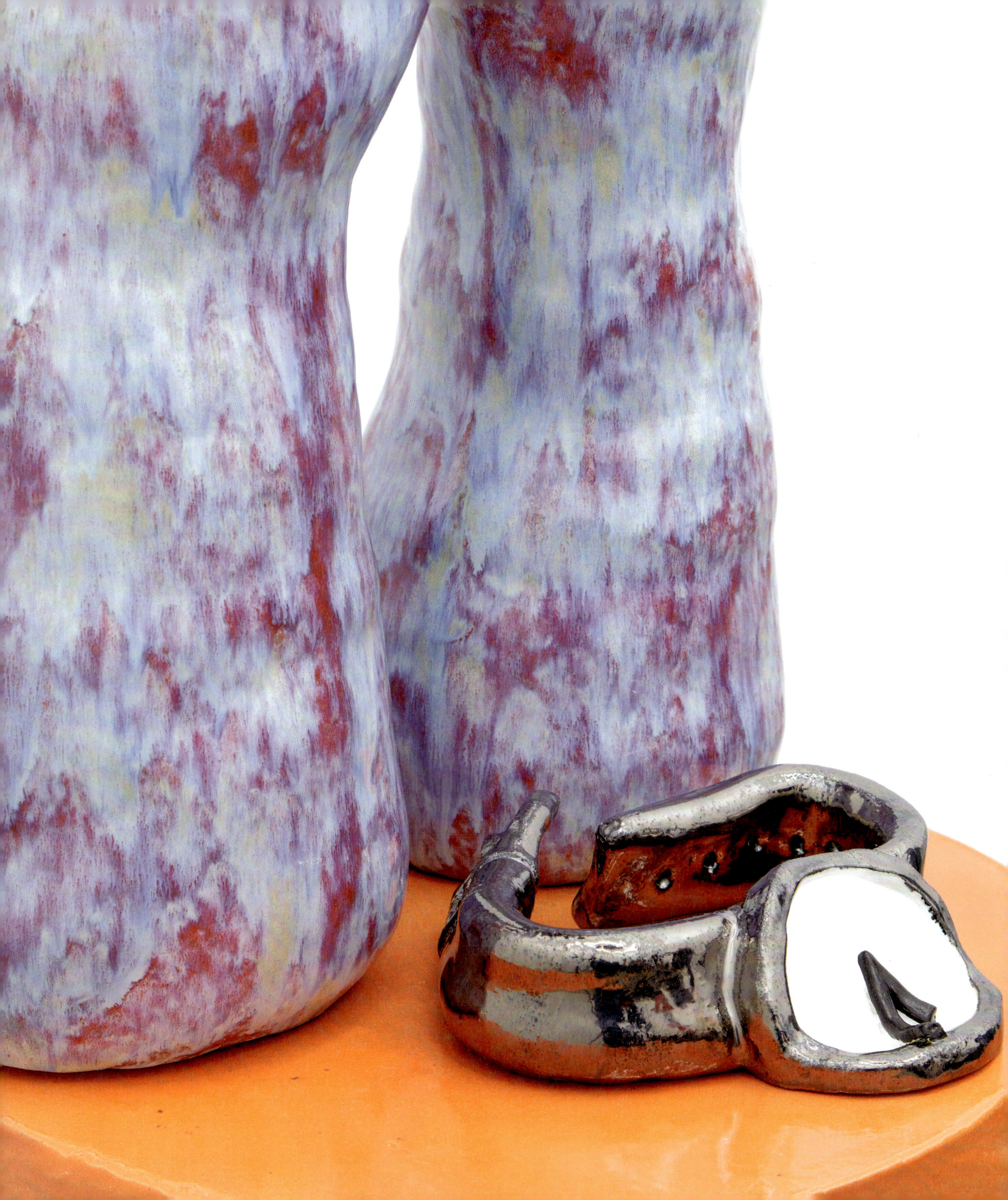

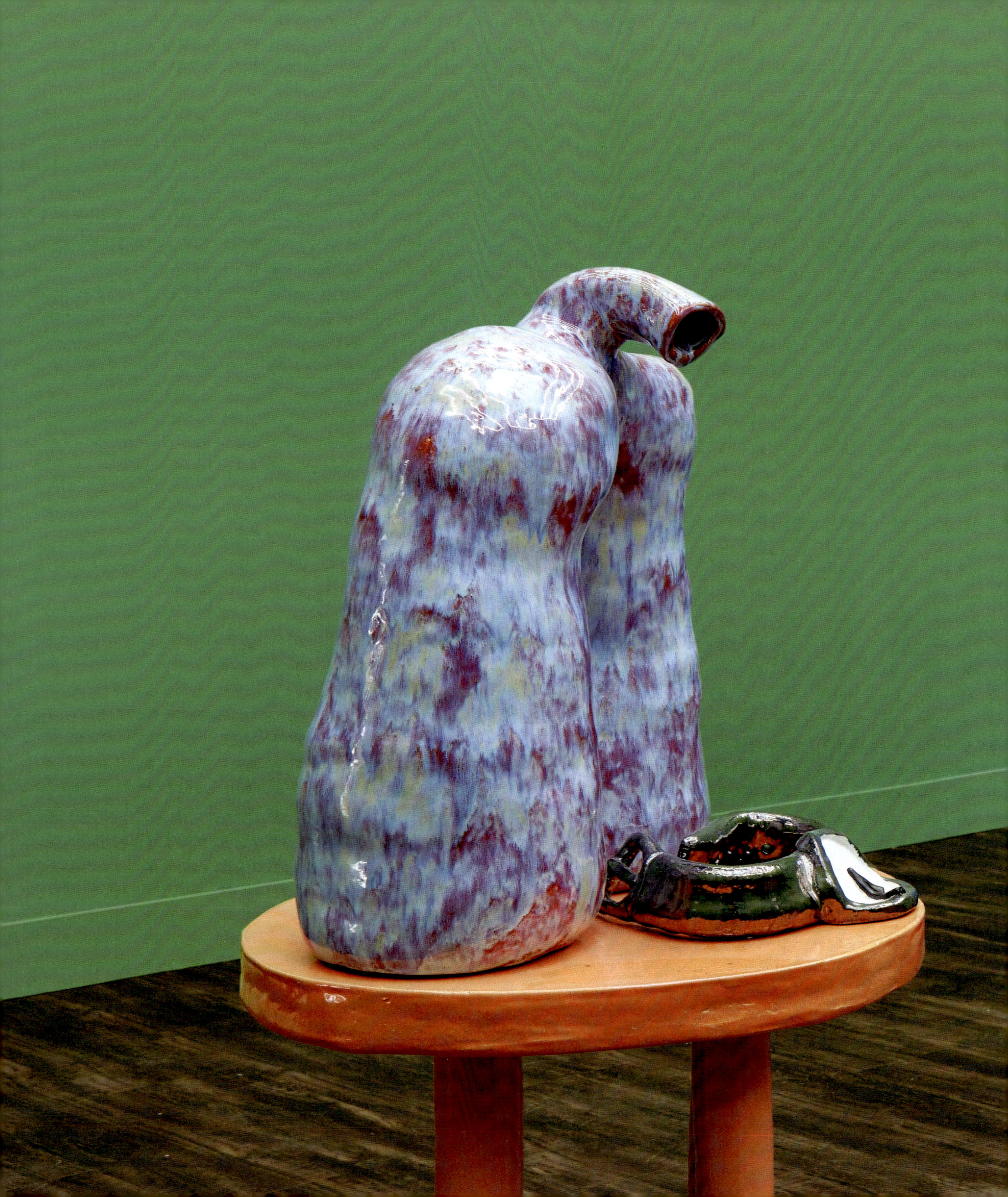

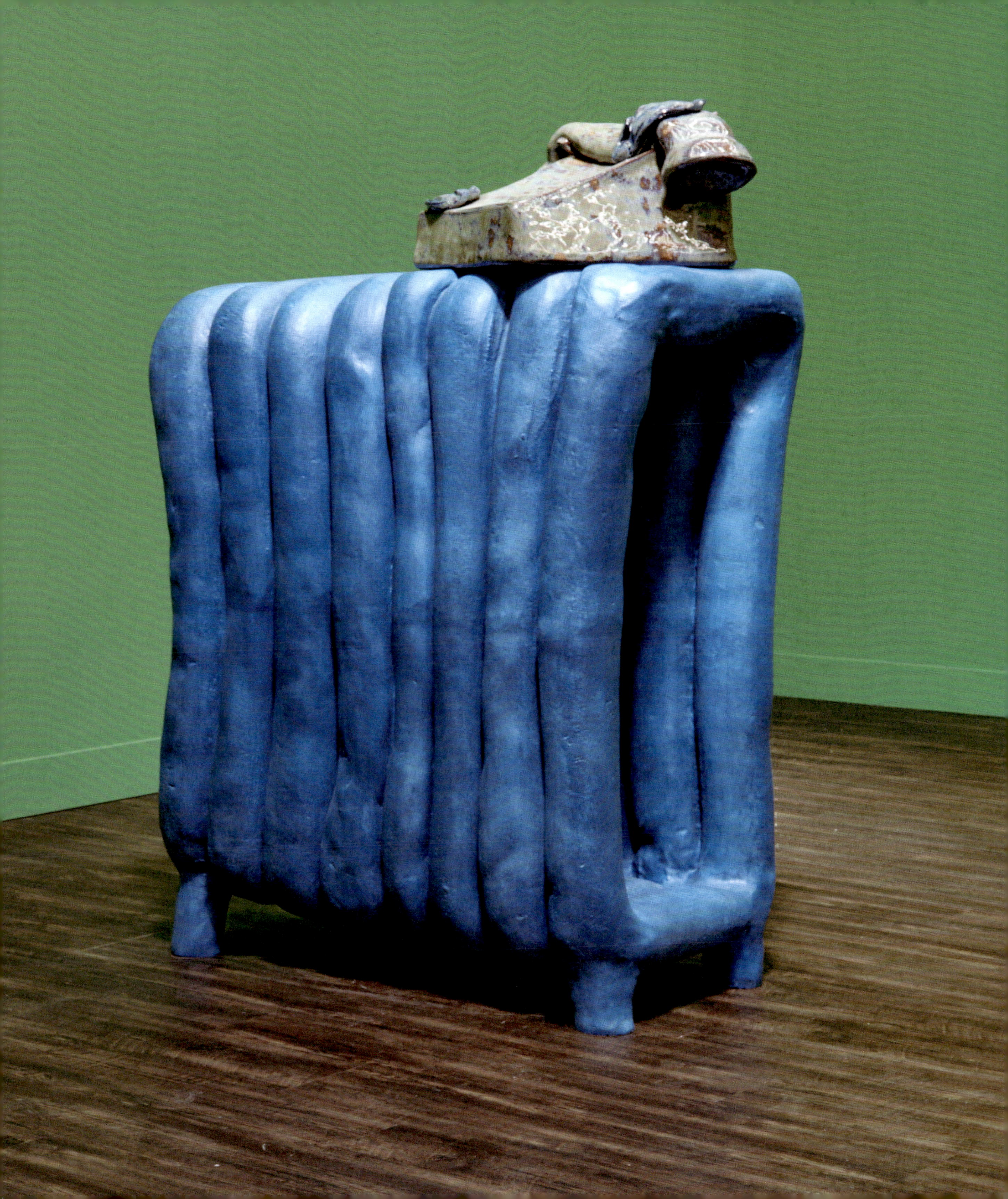

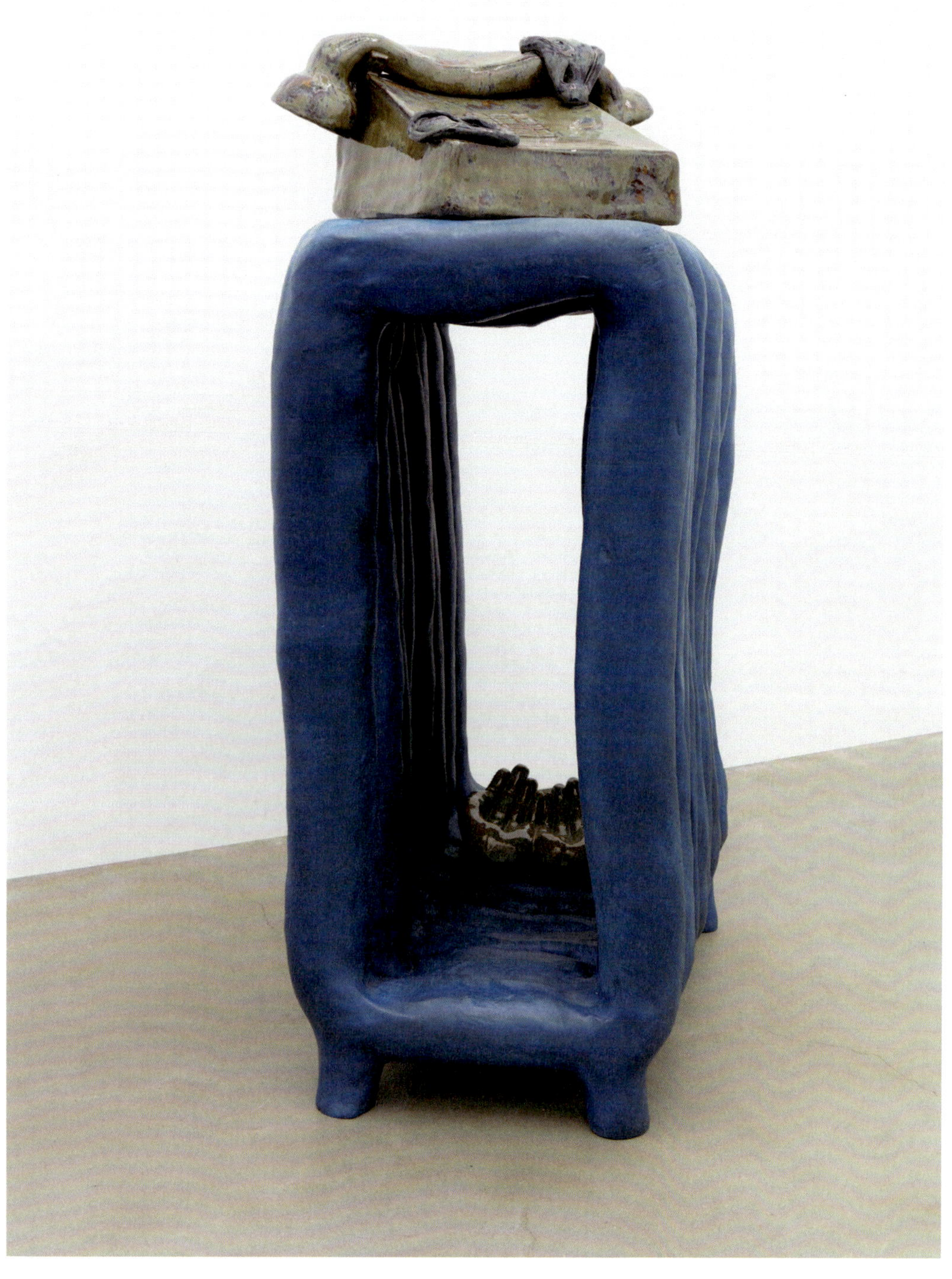

Awaiting on the good news, 2022. Bronze with glazed ceramics,
50 × 48 × 25 in. (127 × 121.9 × 63.5 cm)

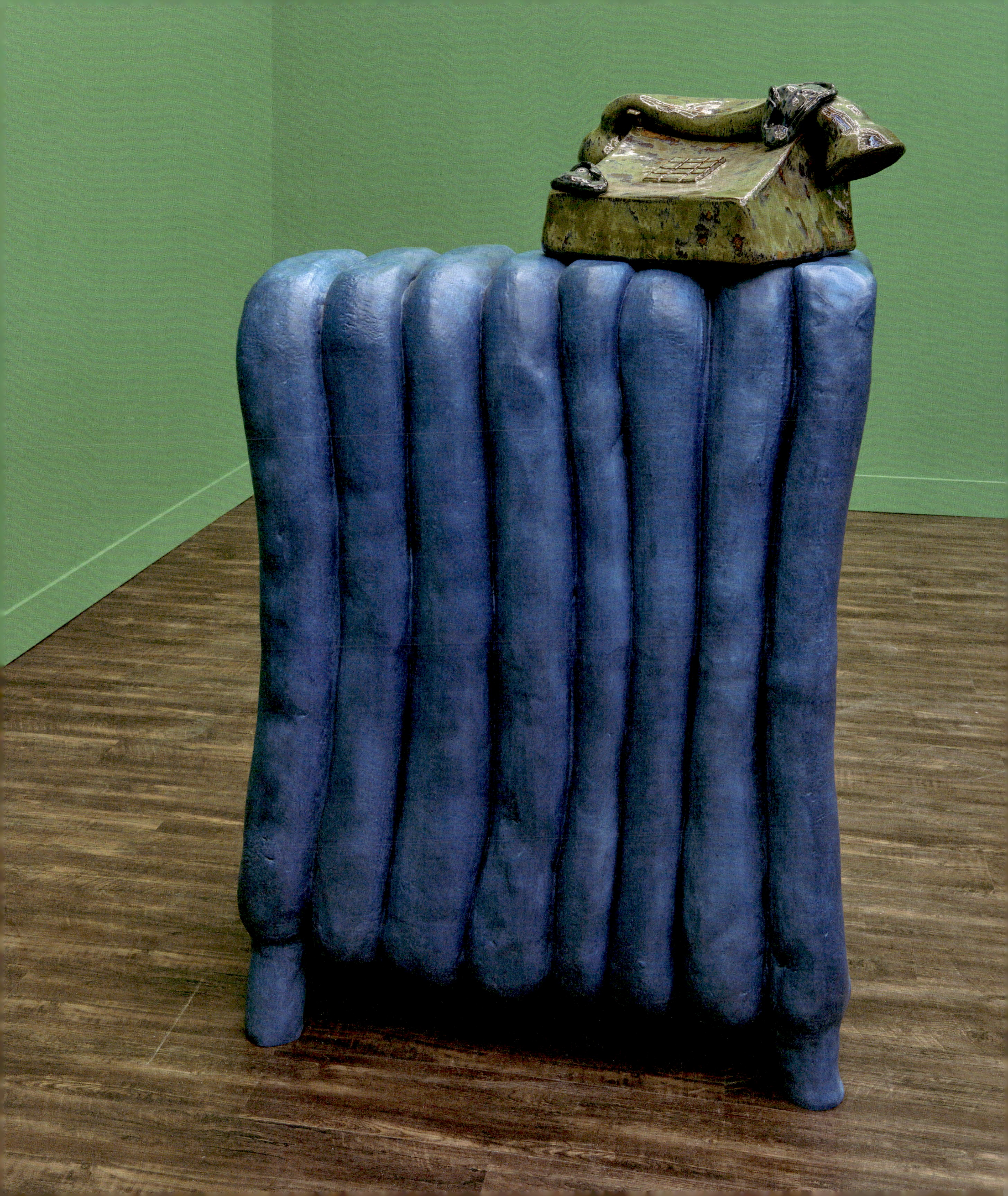

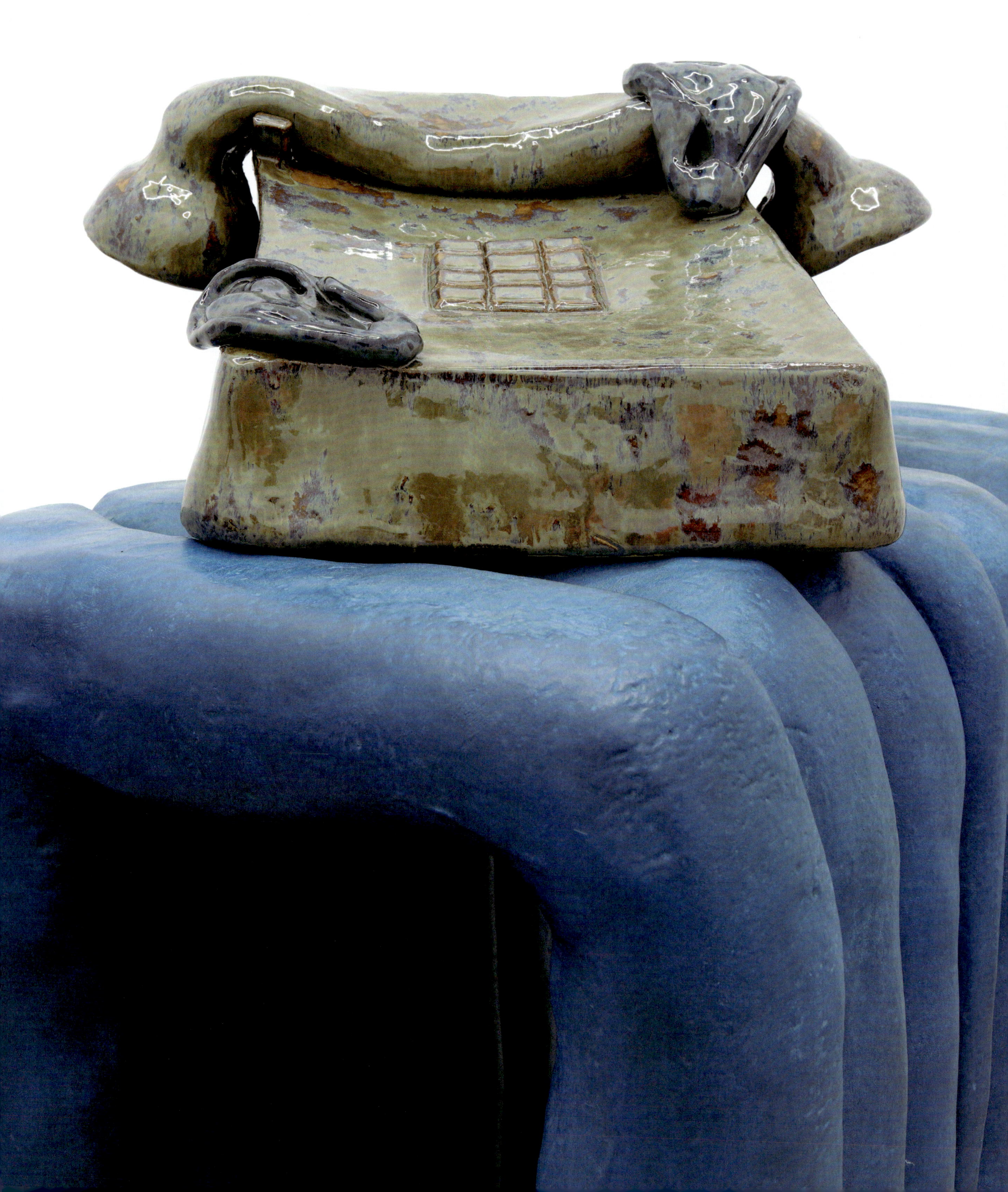

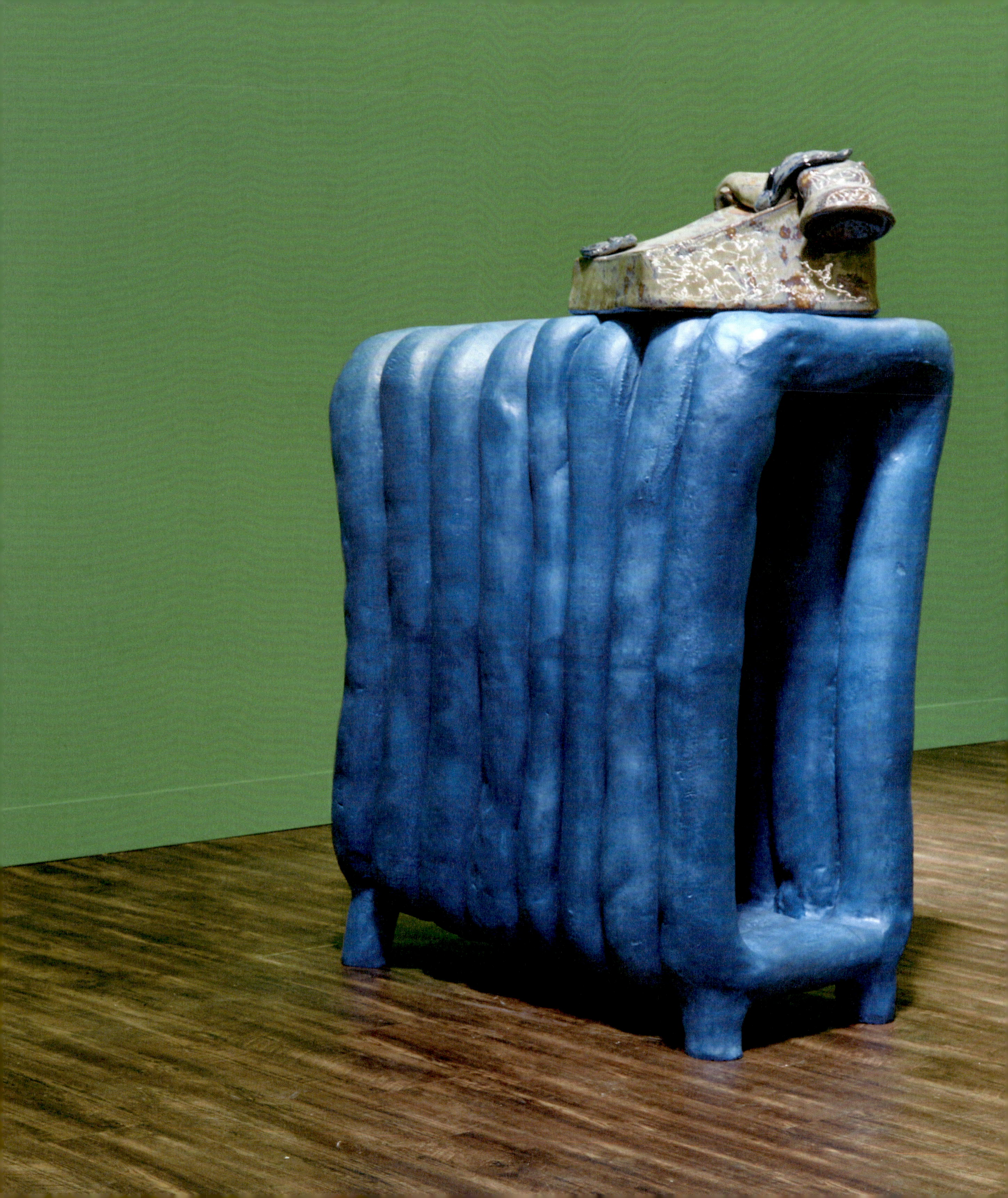

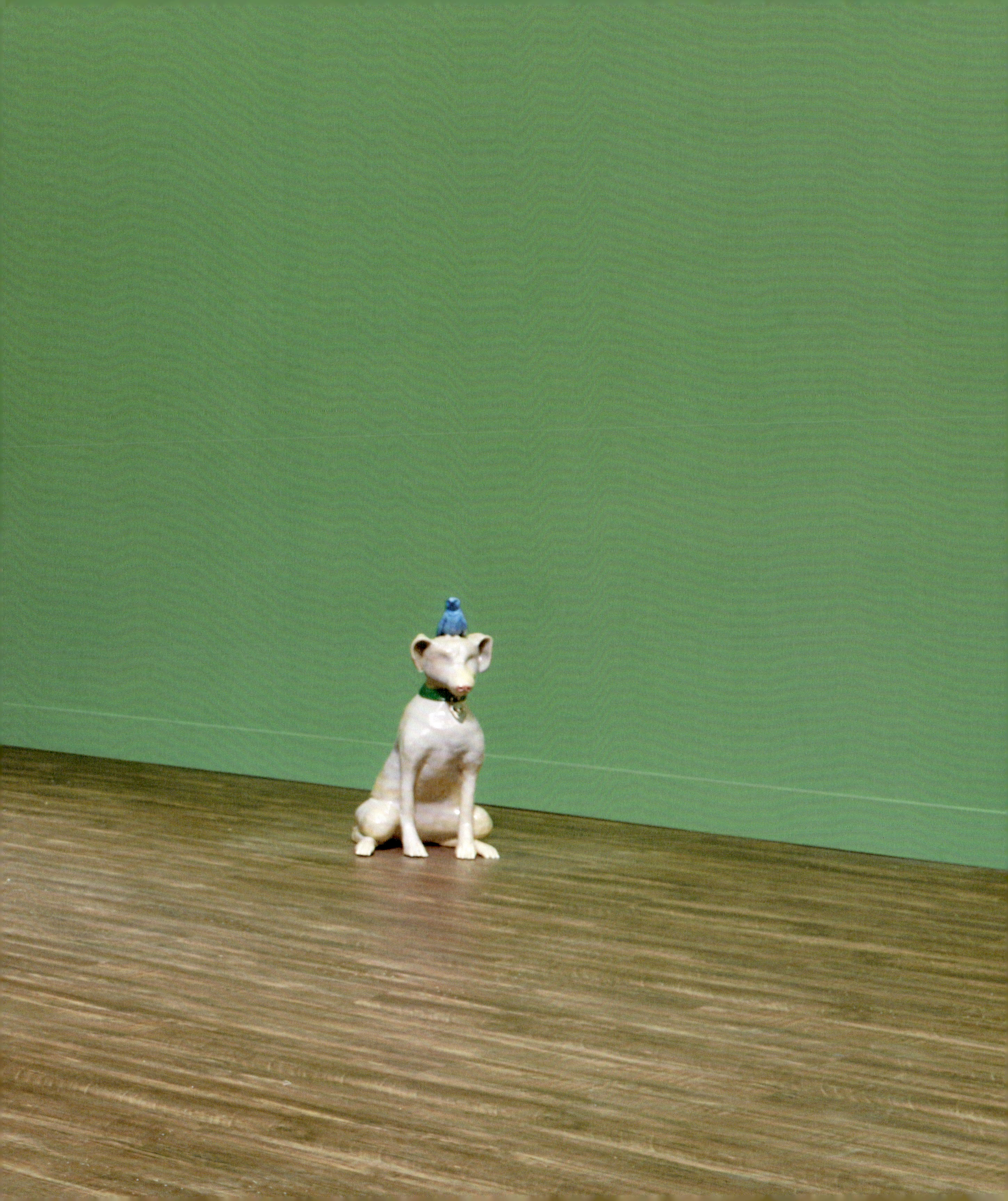

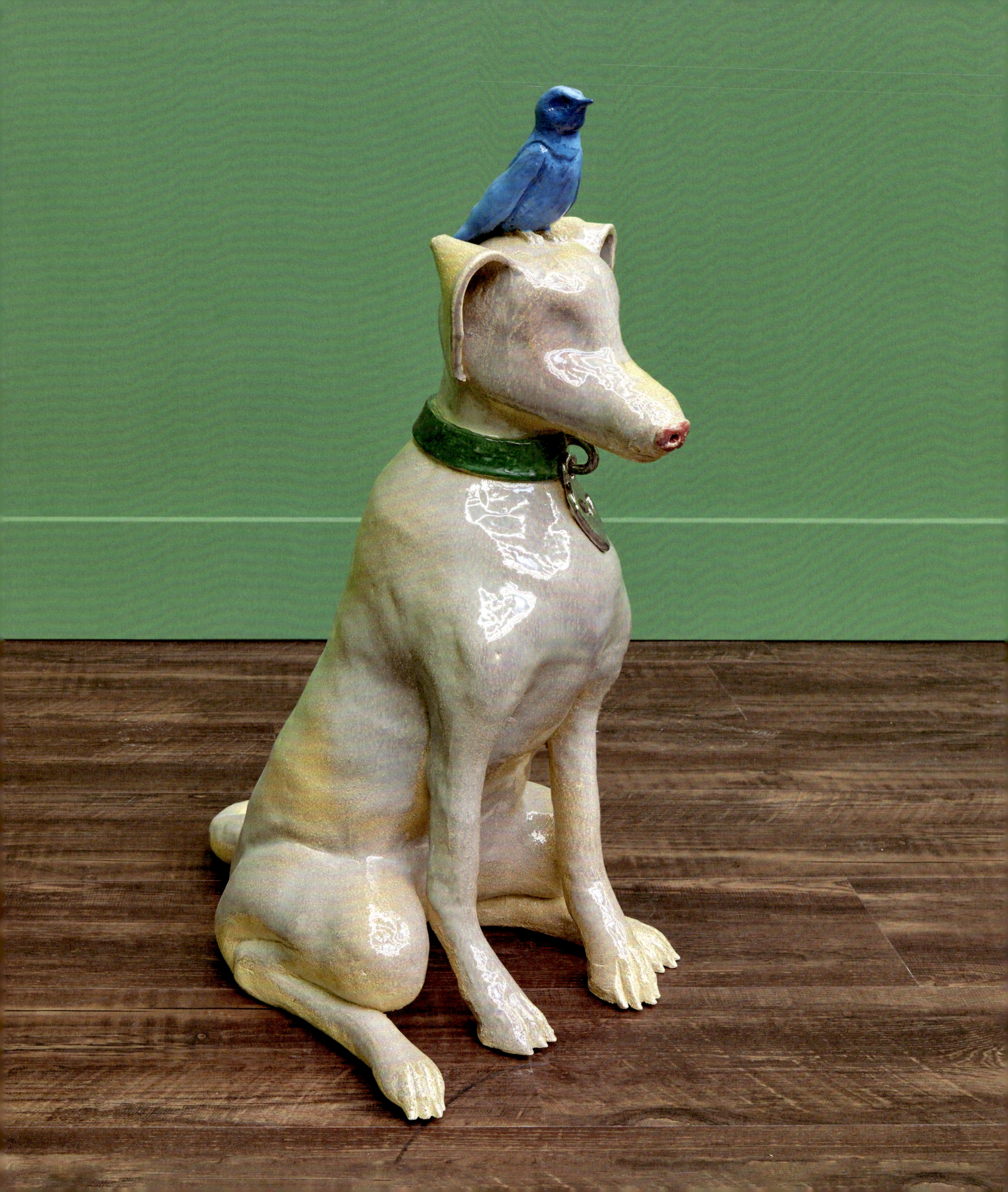

Sentient sunshine, 2022. Ceramic and glaze,
27 × 14 × 15 in. (68.6 × 35.6 × 38.1 cm)

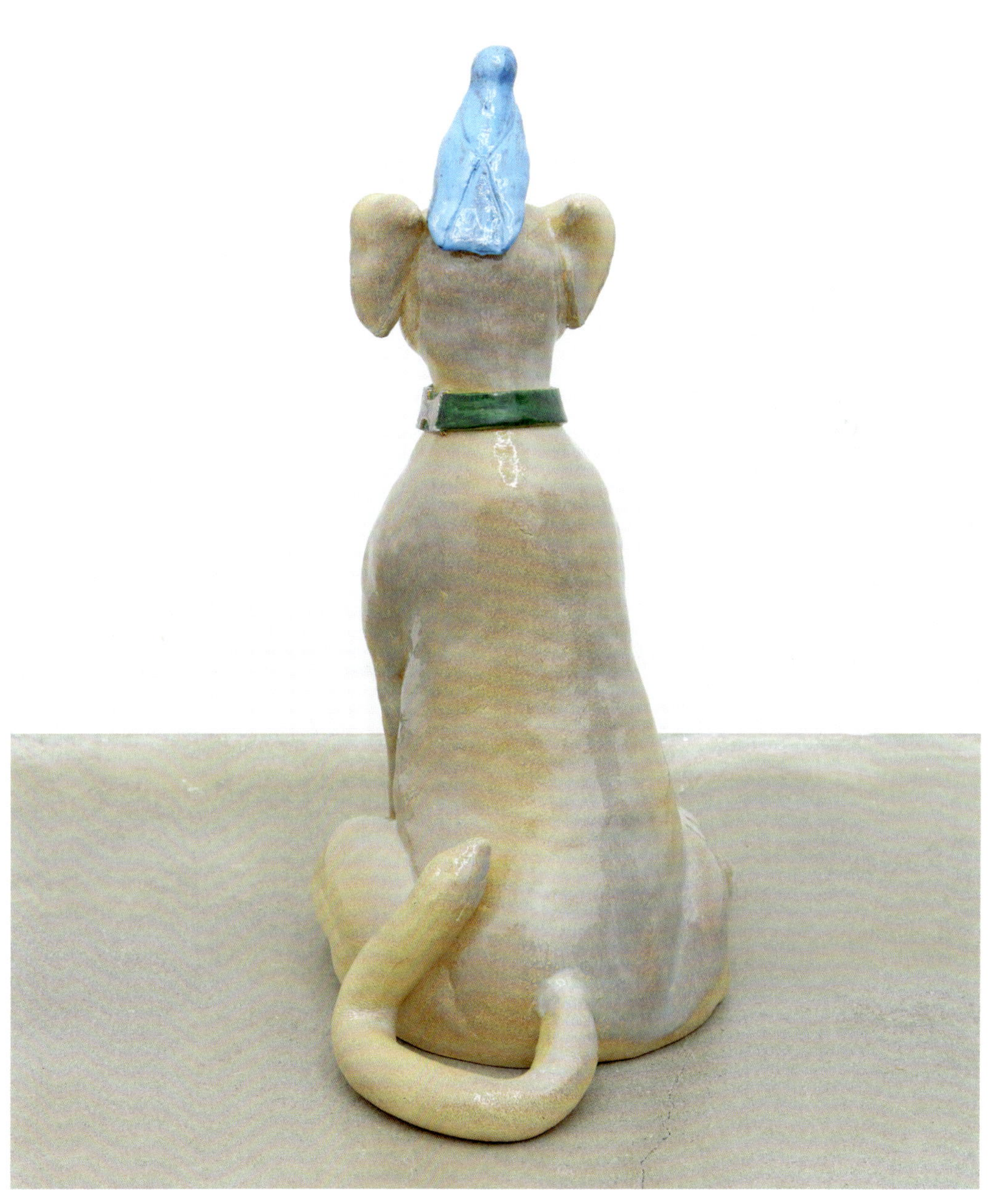

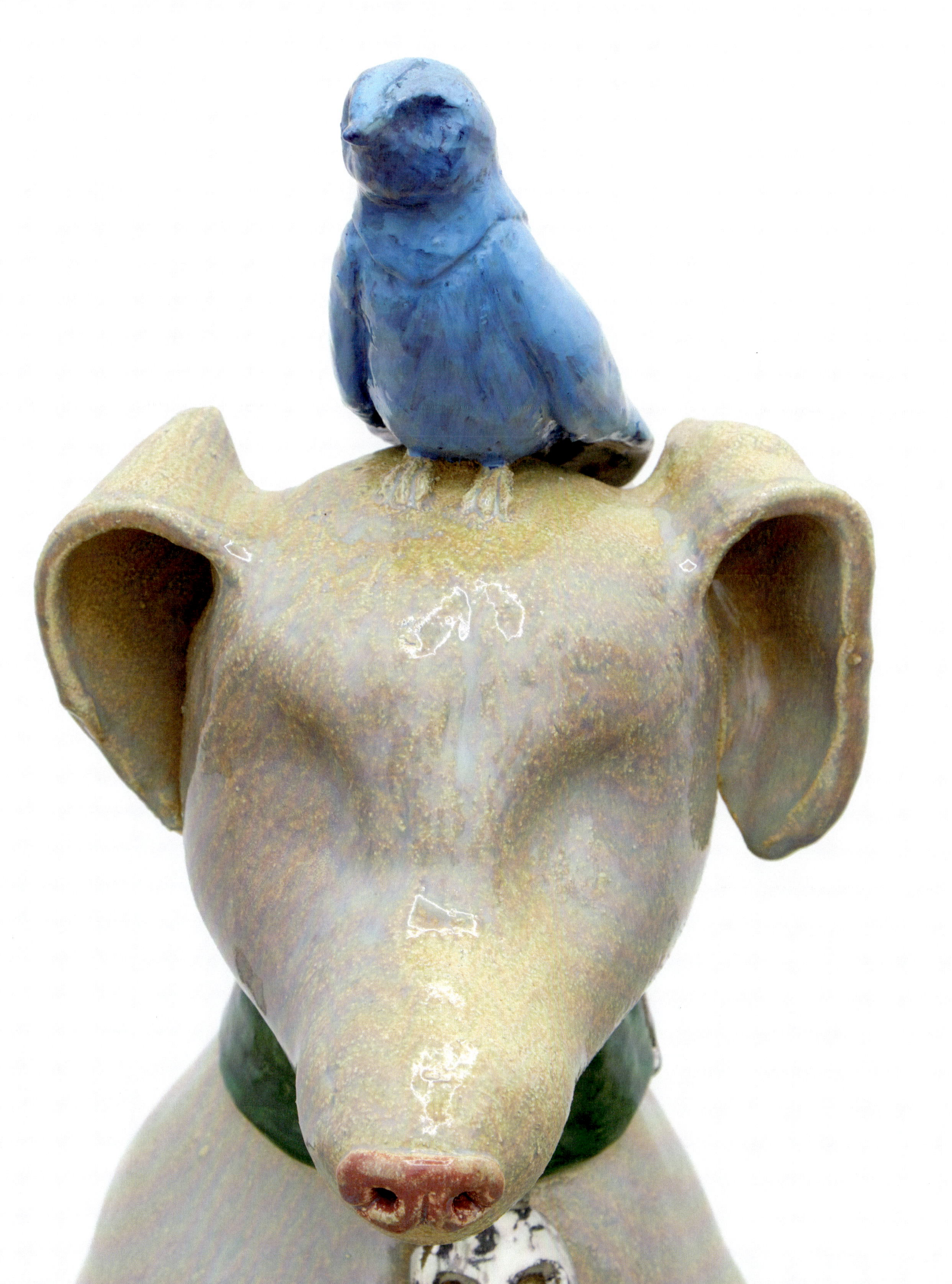

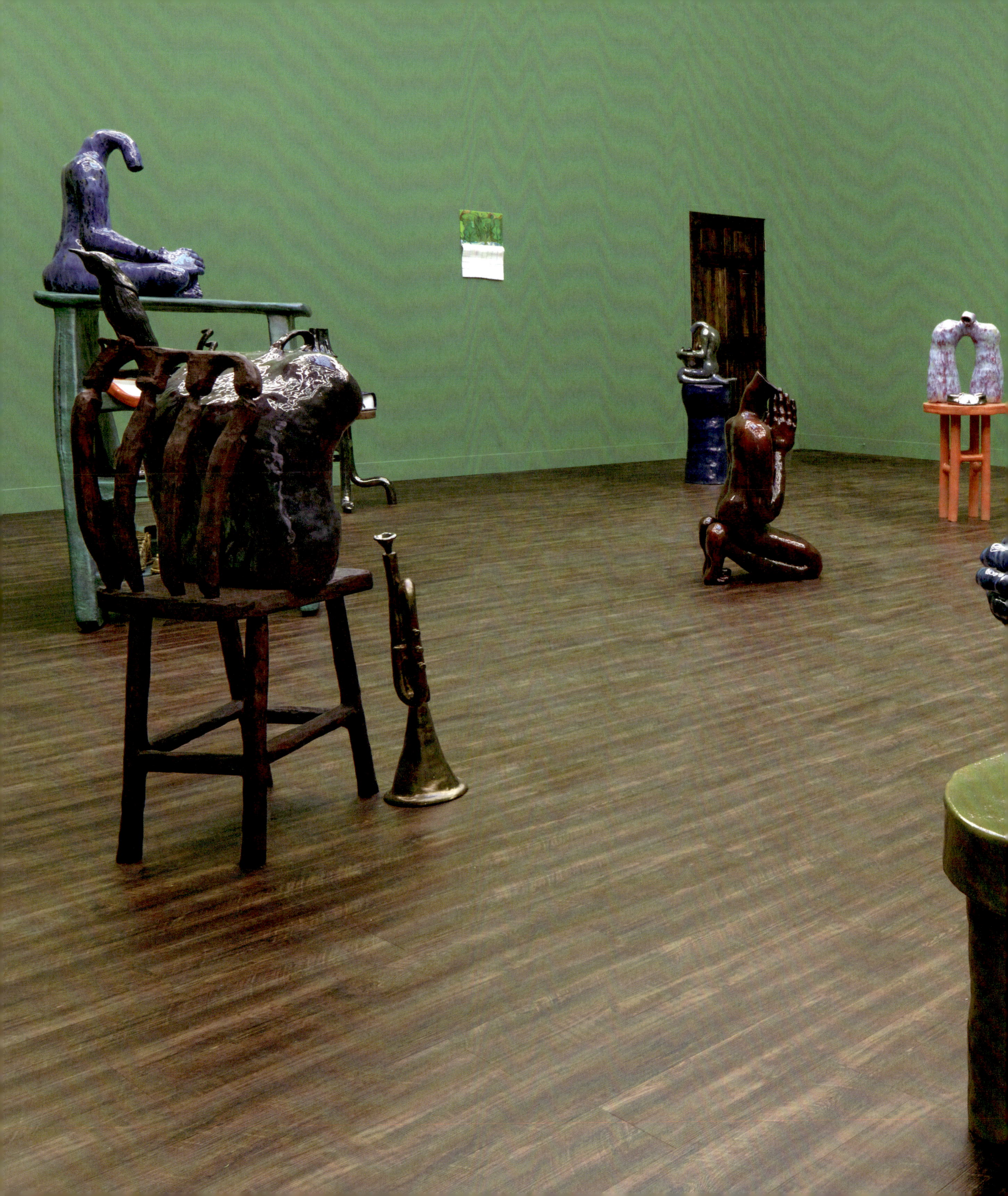

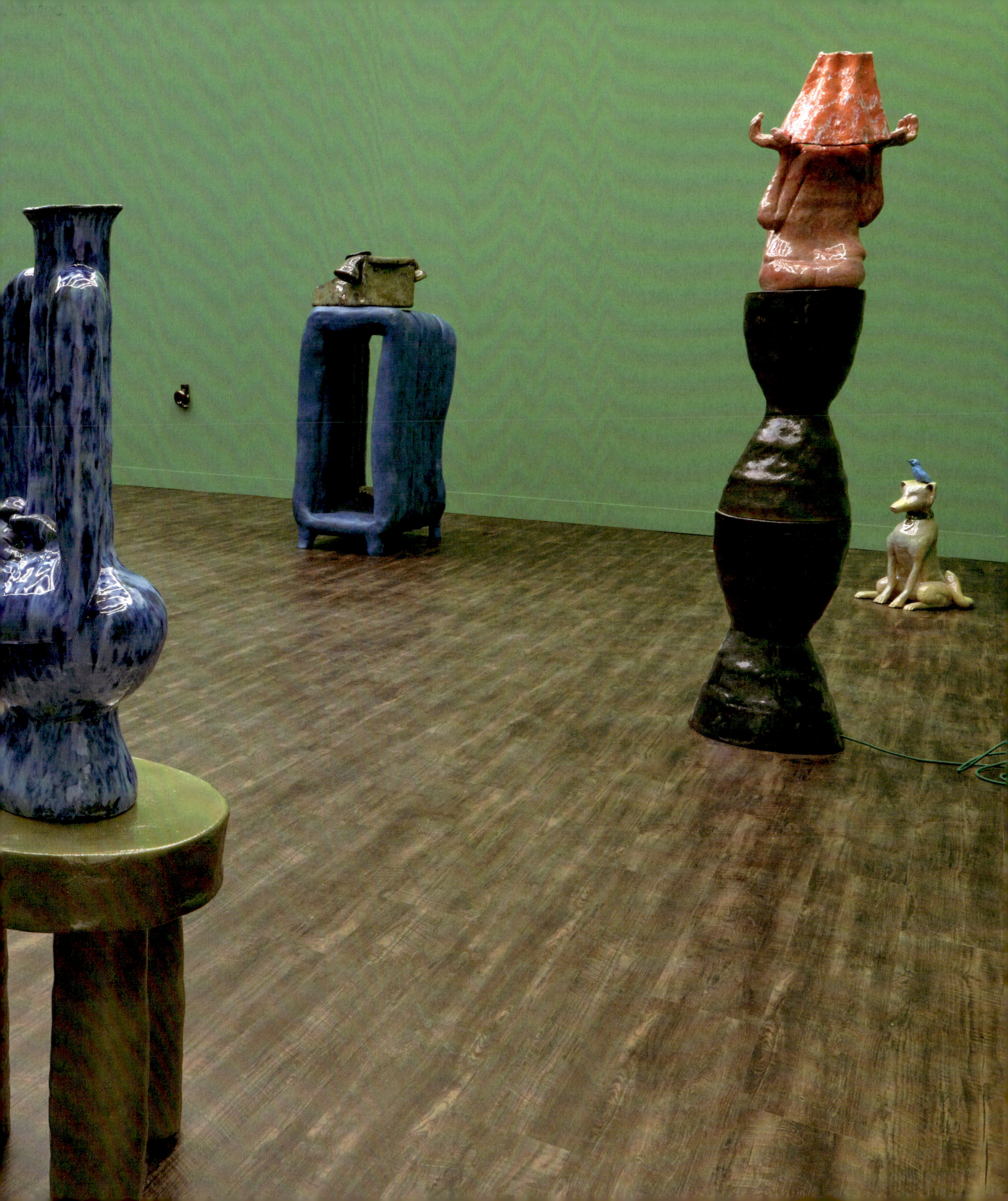

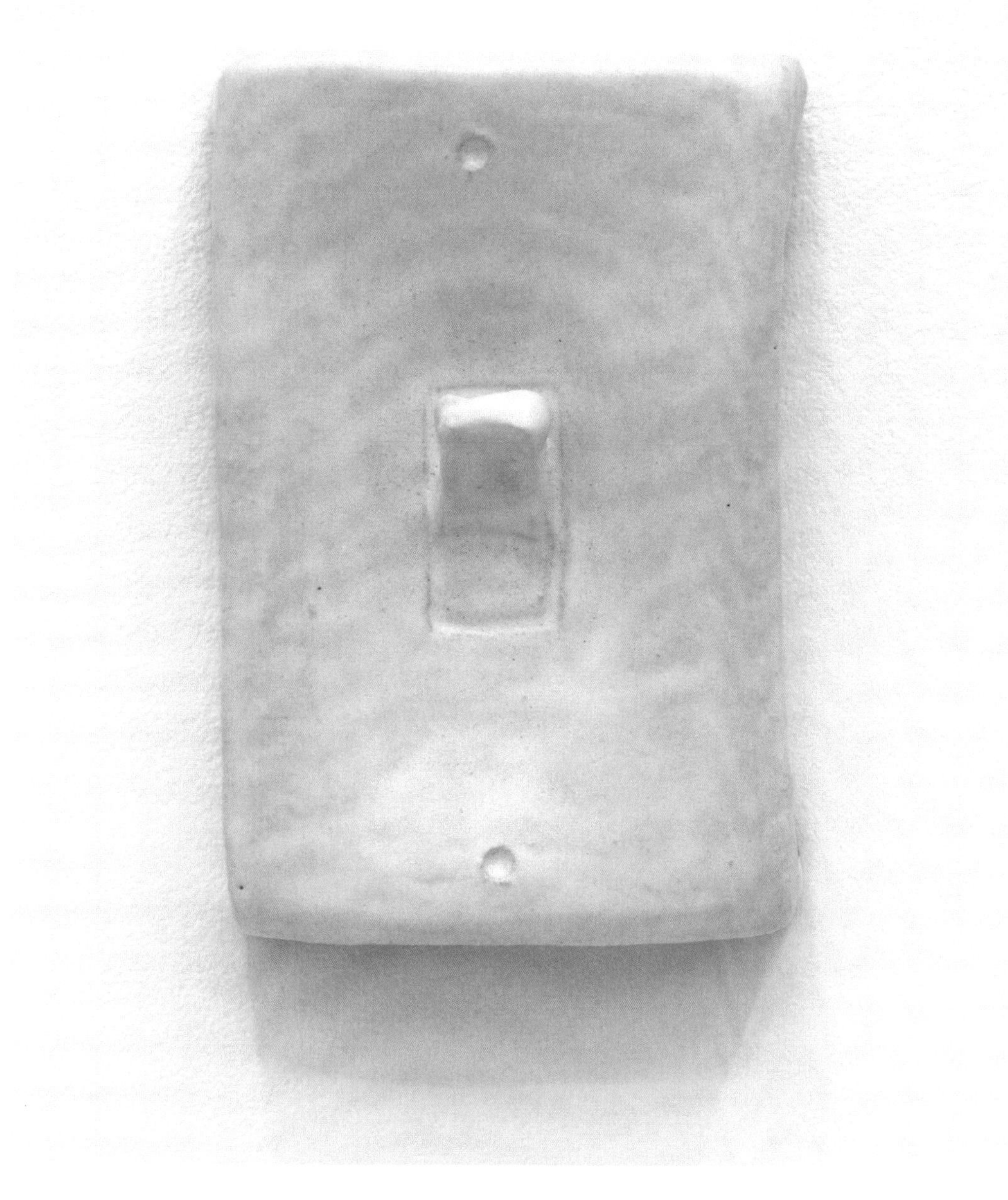

Keep on keepin on, 2022. Ceramic and glaze,
6 × 4 × 1 in. (15.2 × 10.2 × 2.5 cm)

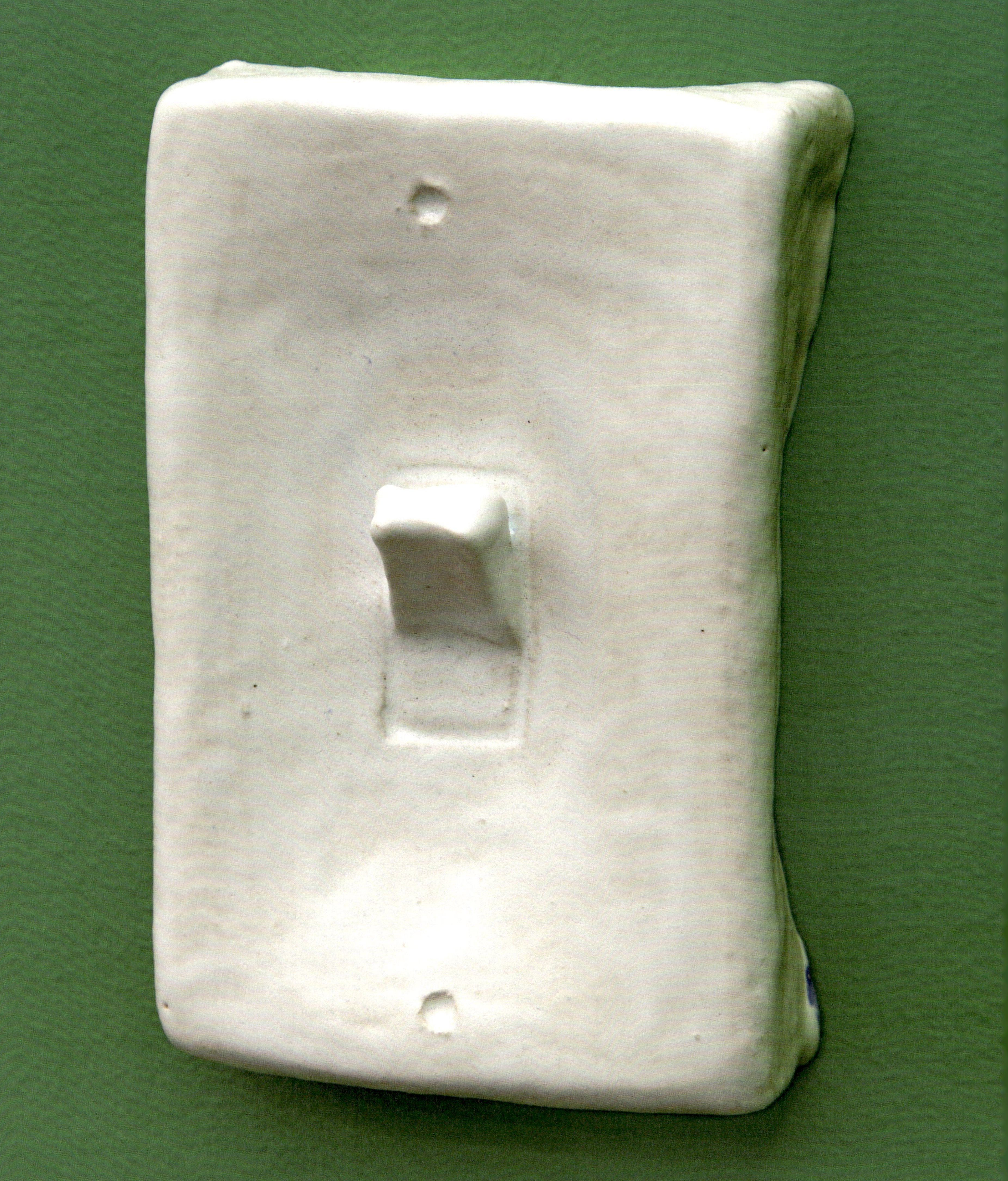

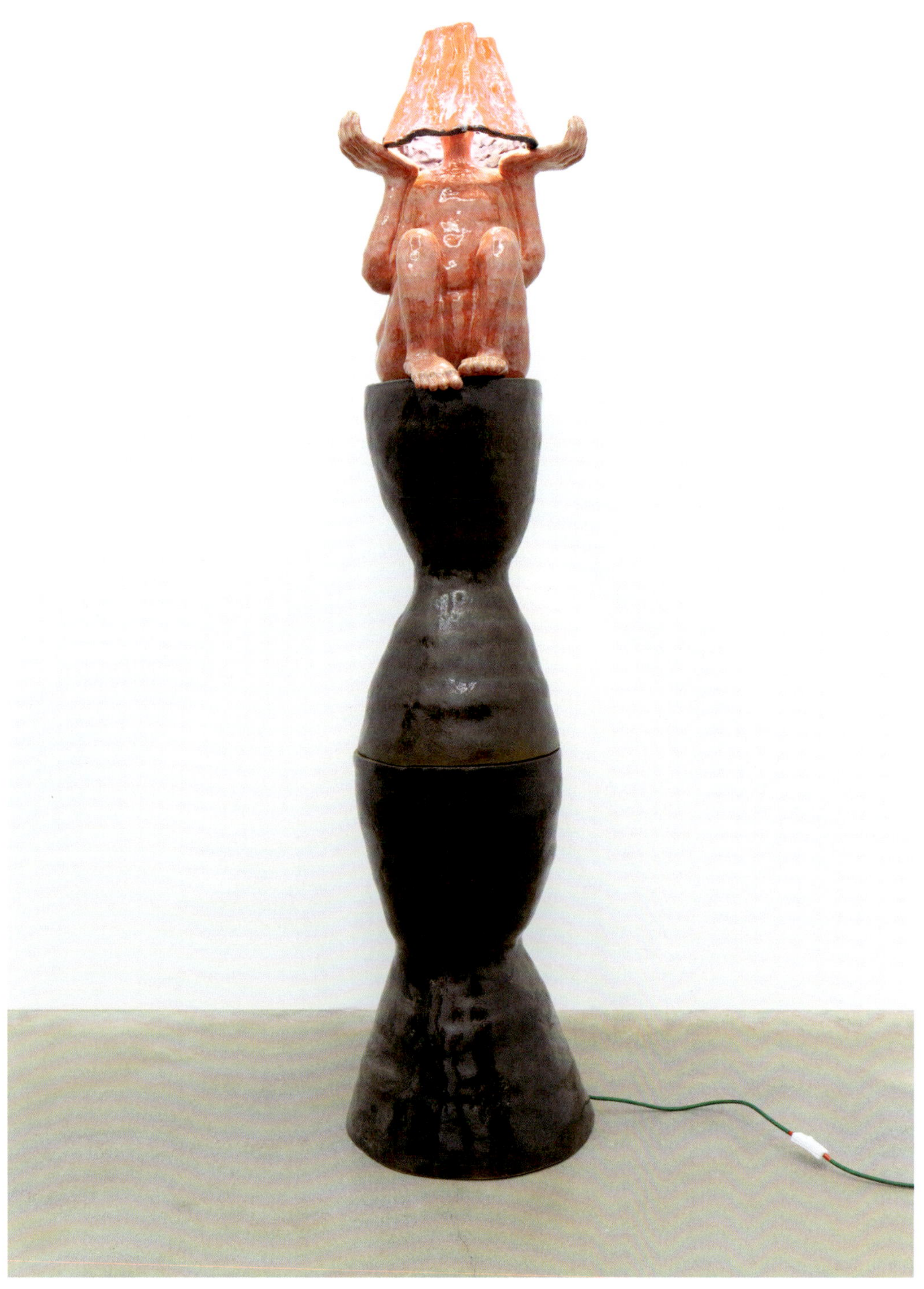

Keeping the light on, 2022. Ceramic, glaze, and lightbulb with wire,
70 × 20 × 20 in. (177.8 × 50.8 × 50.8 cm)

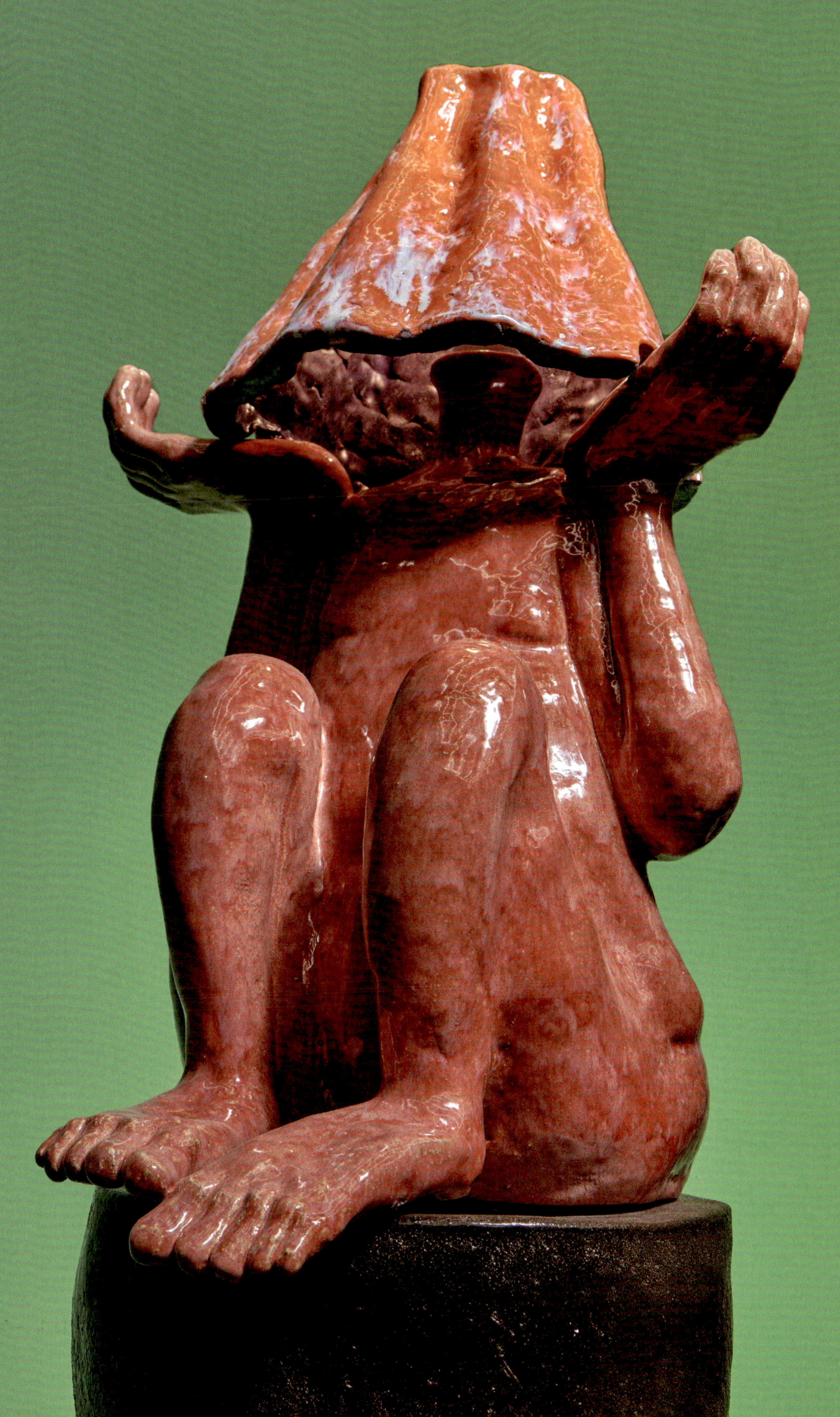

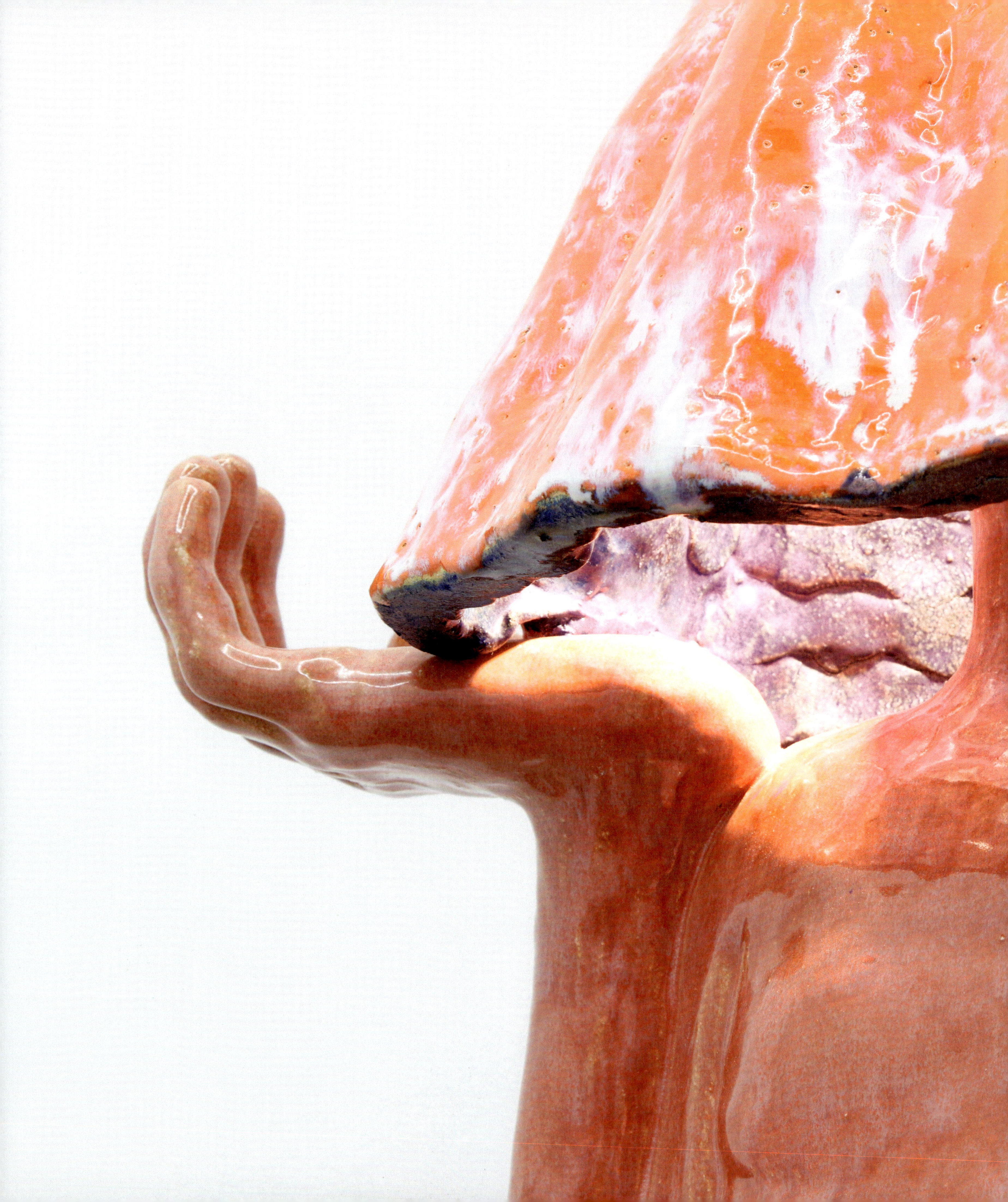

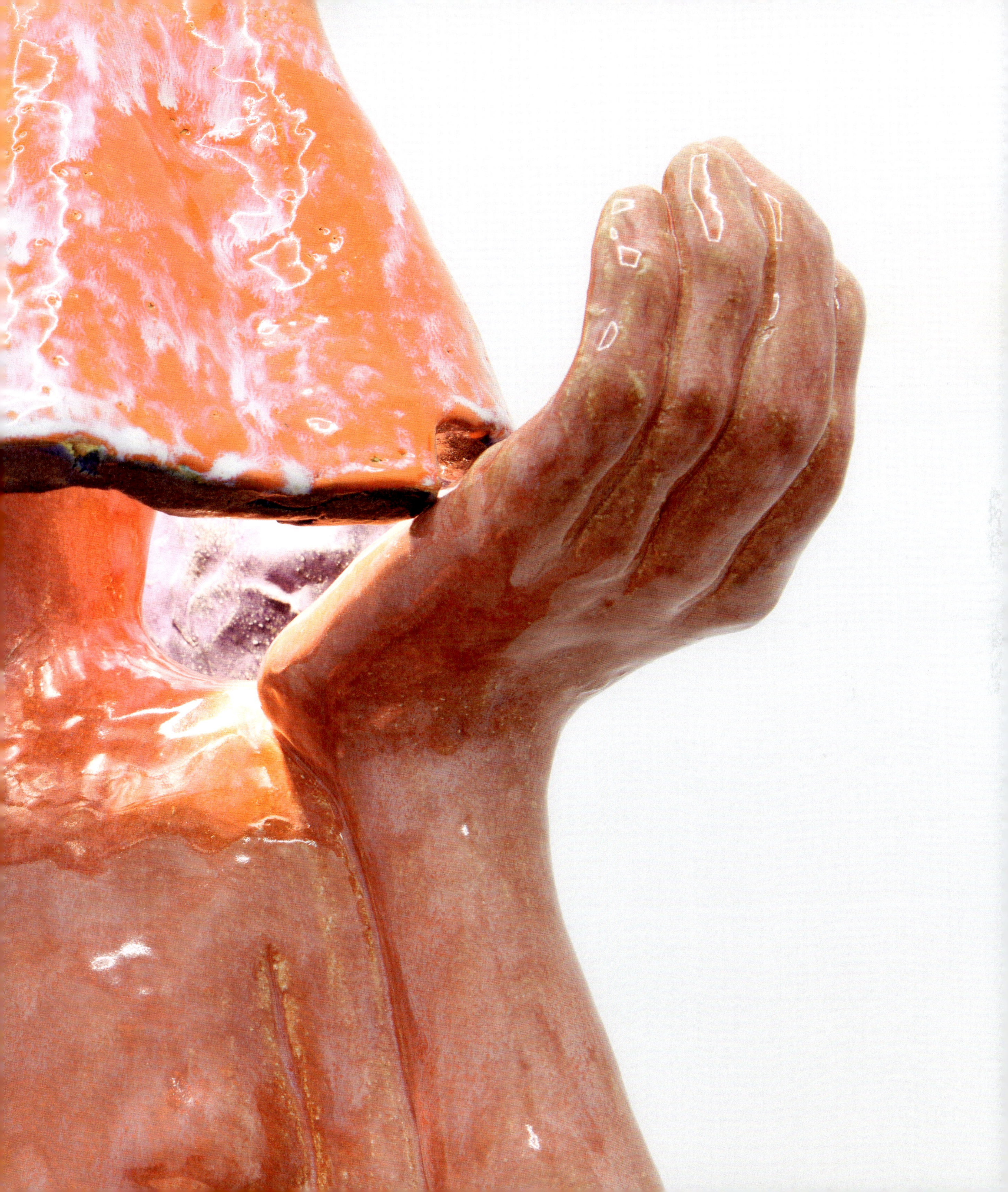

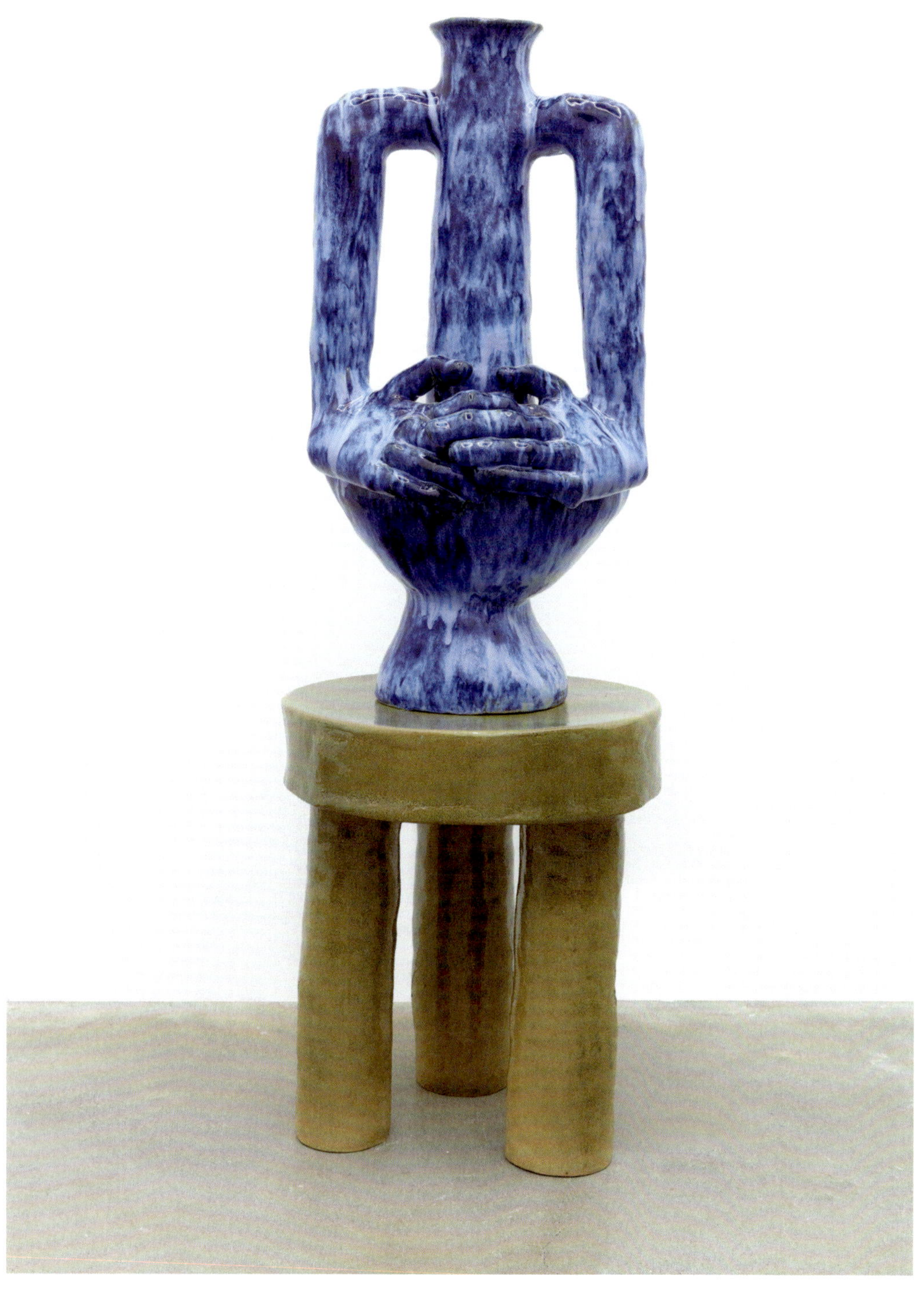

Treading water, 2022. Ceramic and glaze,
53 × 17½ × 17½ in. (134.6 × 44.5 × 44.5 cm)

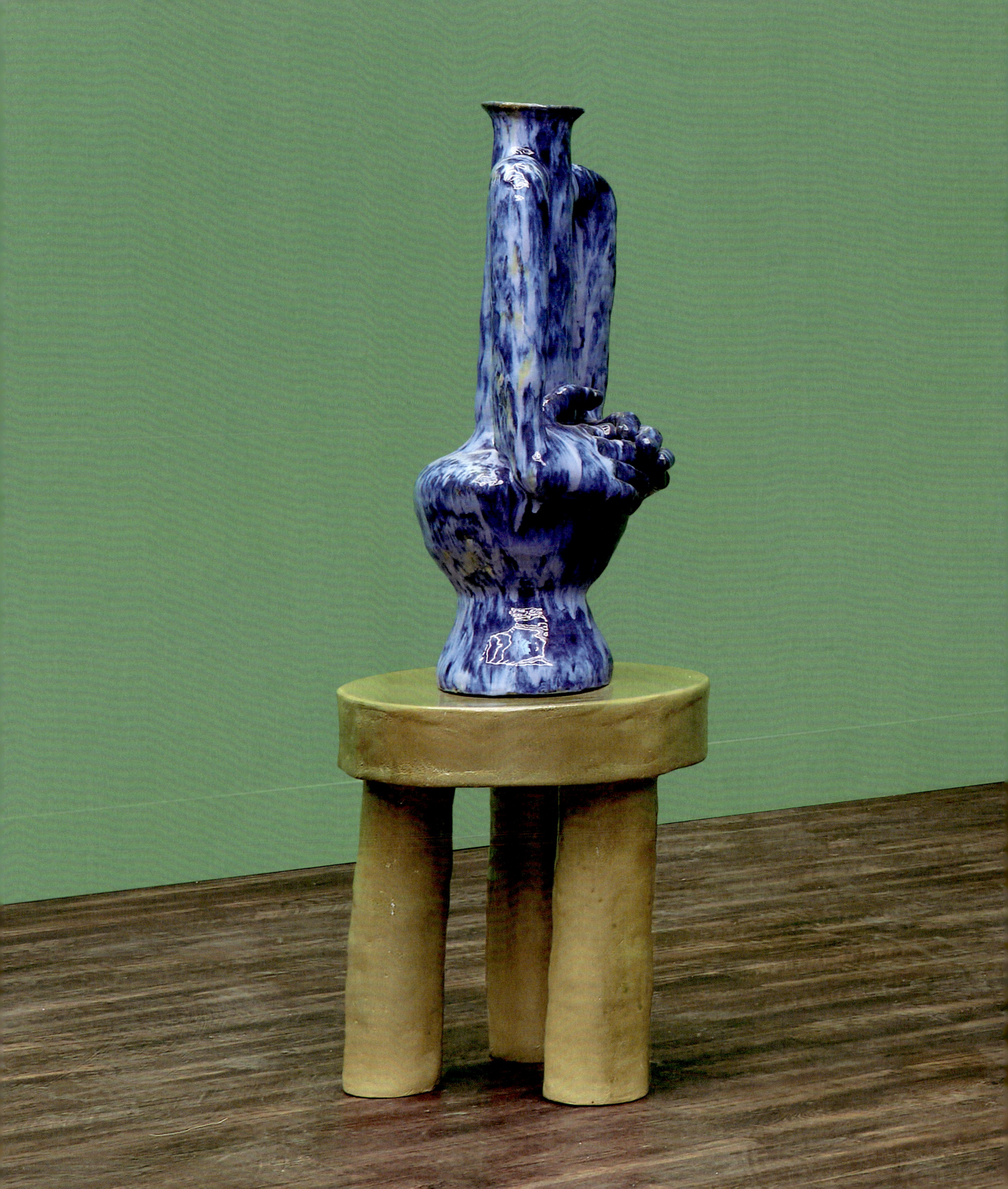

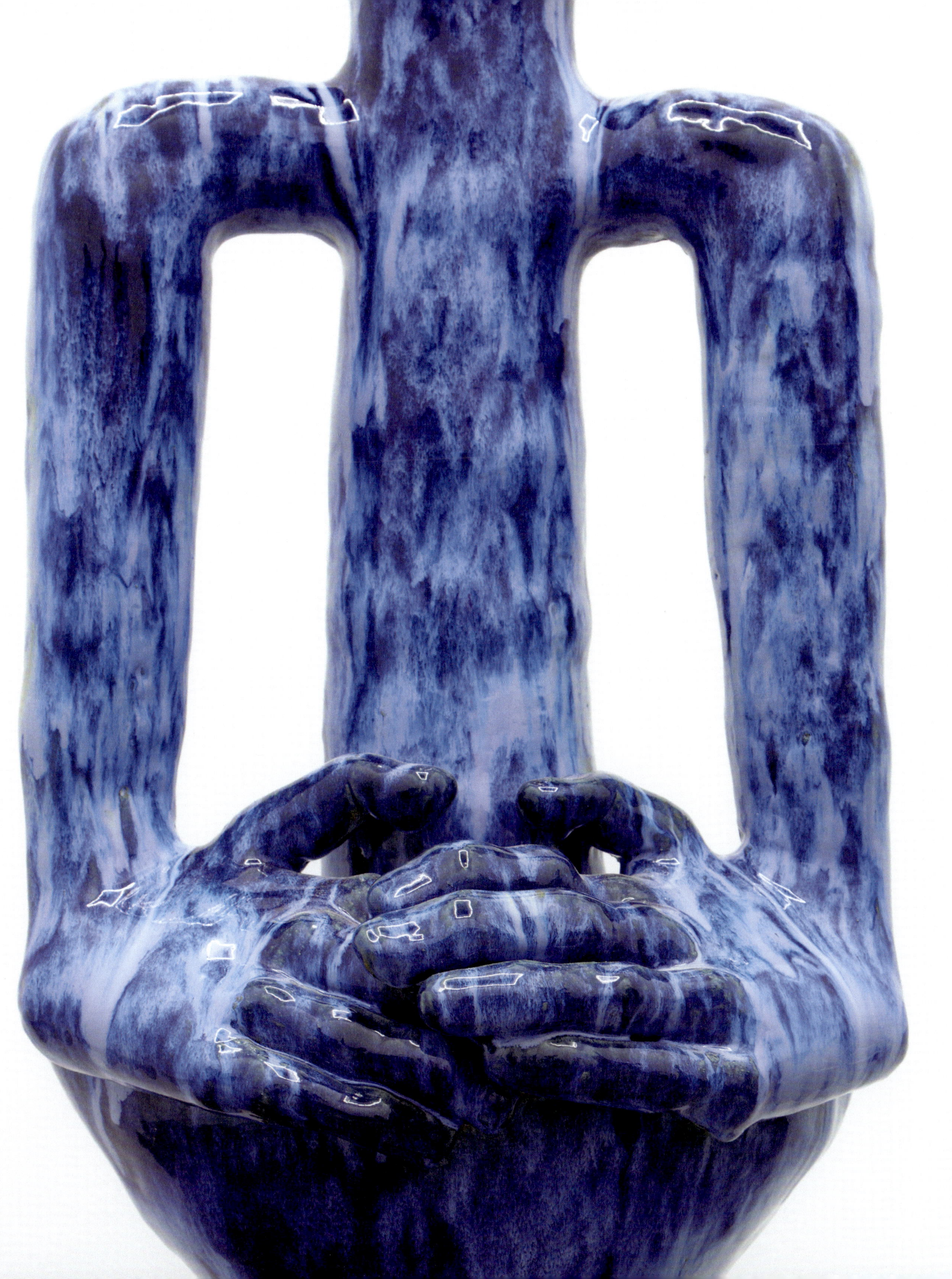

Follow me, 2022. Ceramic, paint, clock hands, clock motor, and battery,
16 × 16 × 2 in. (40.6 × 40.6 × 5.1 cm)

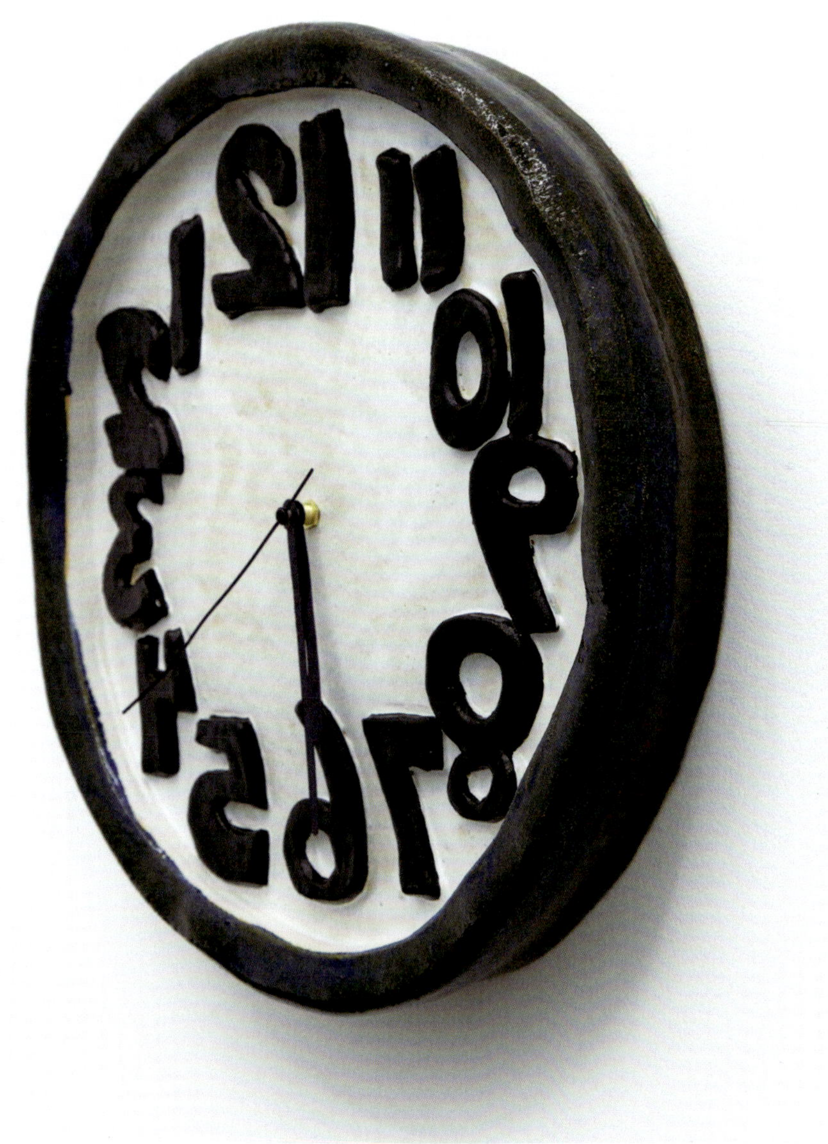

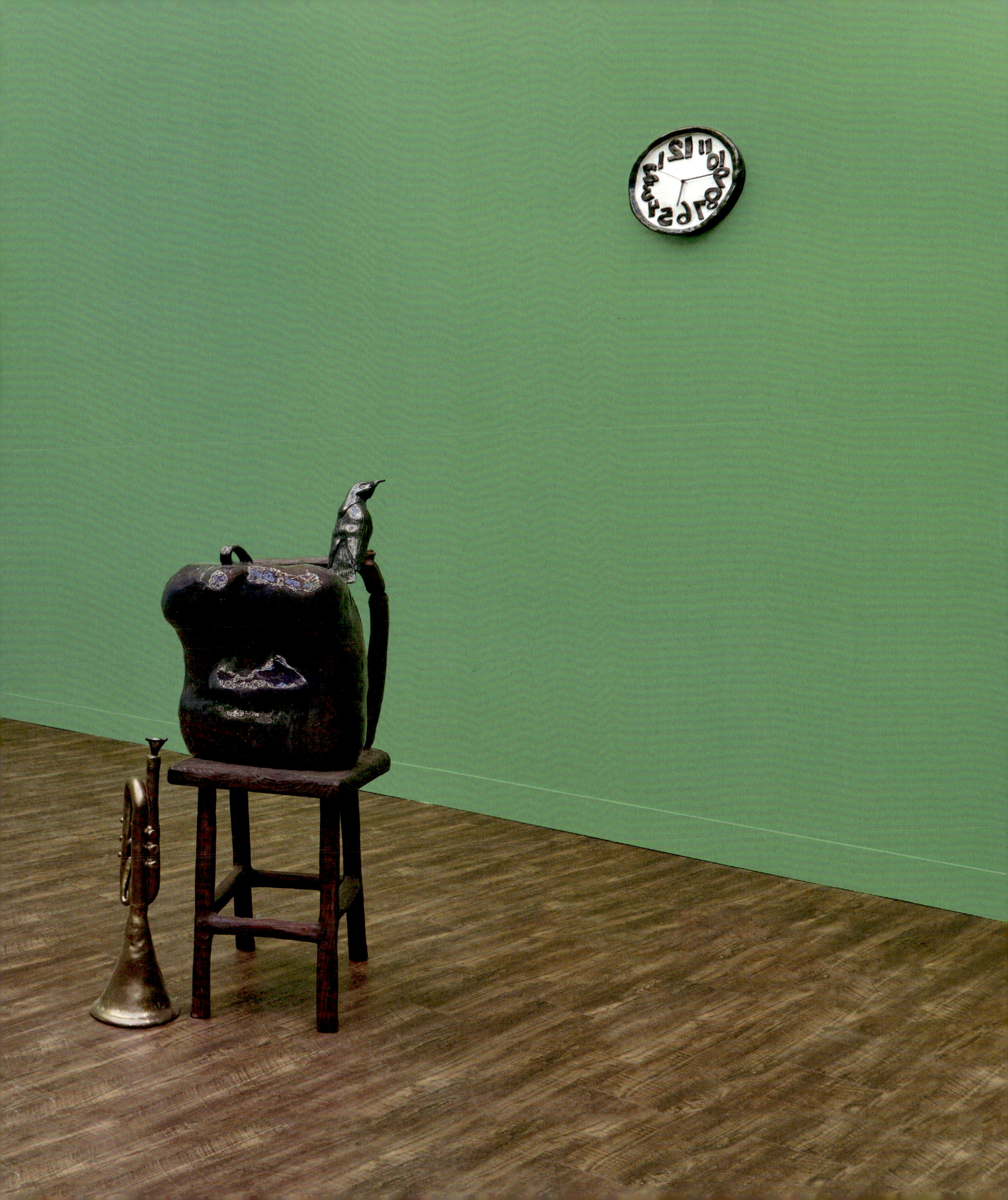

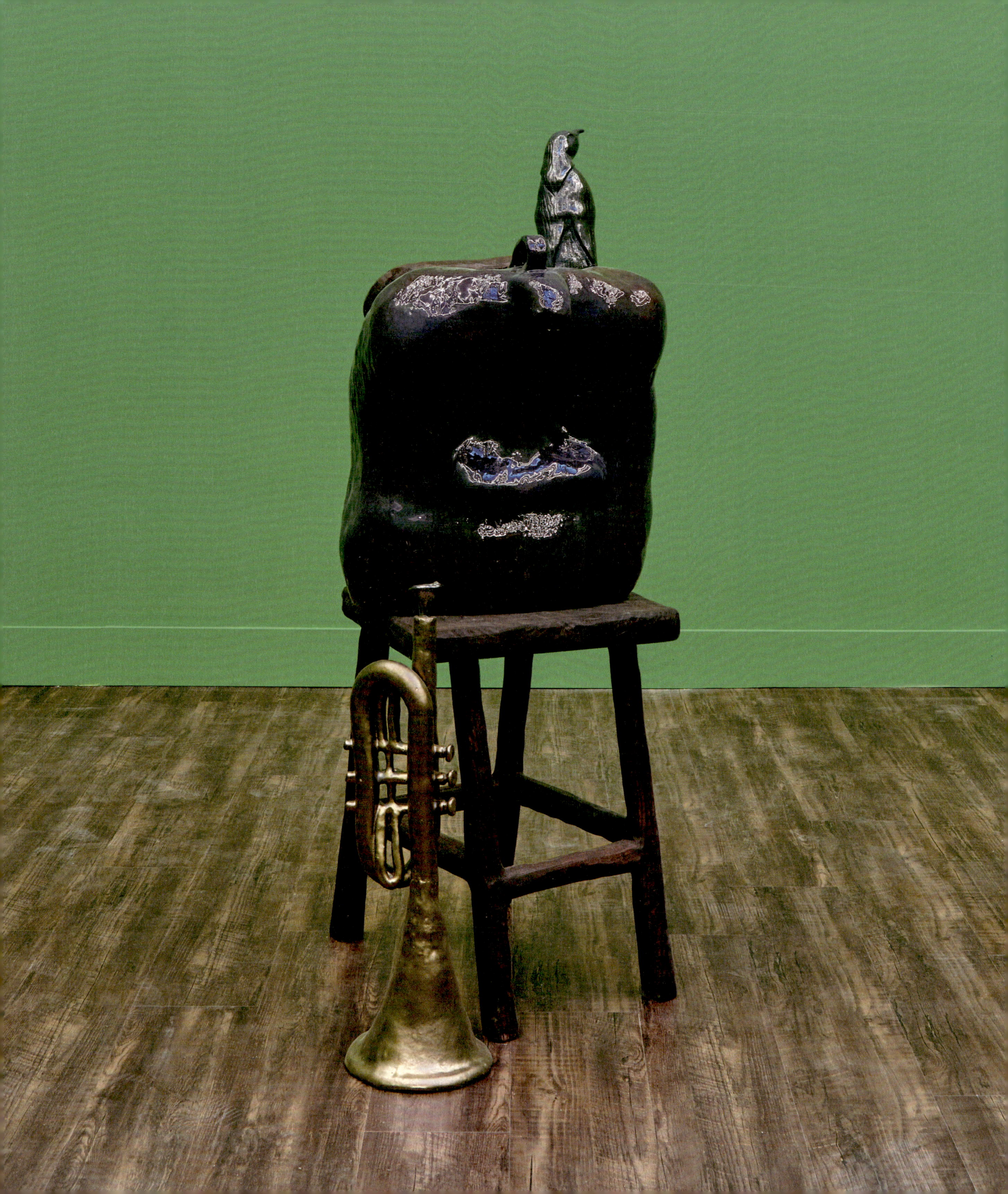

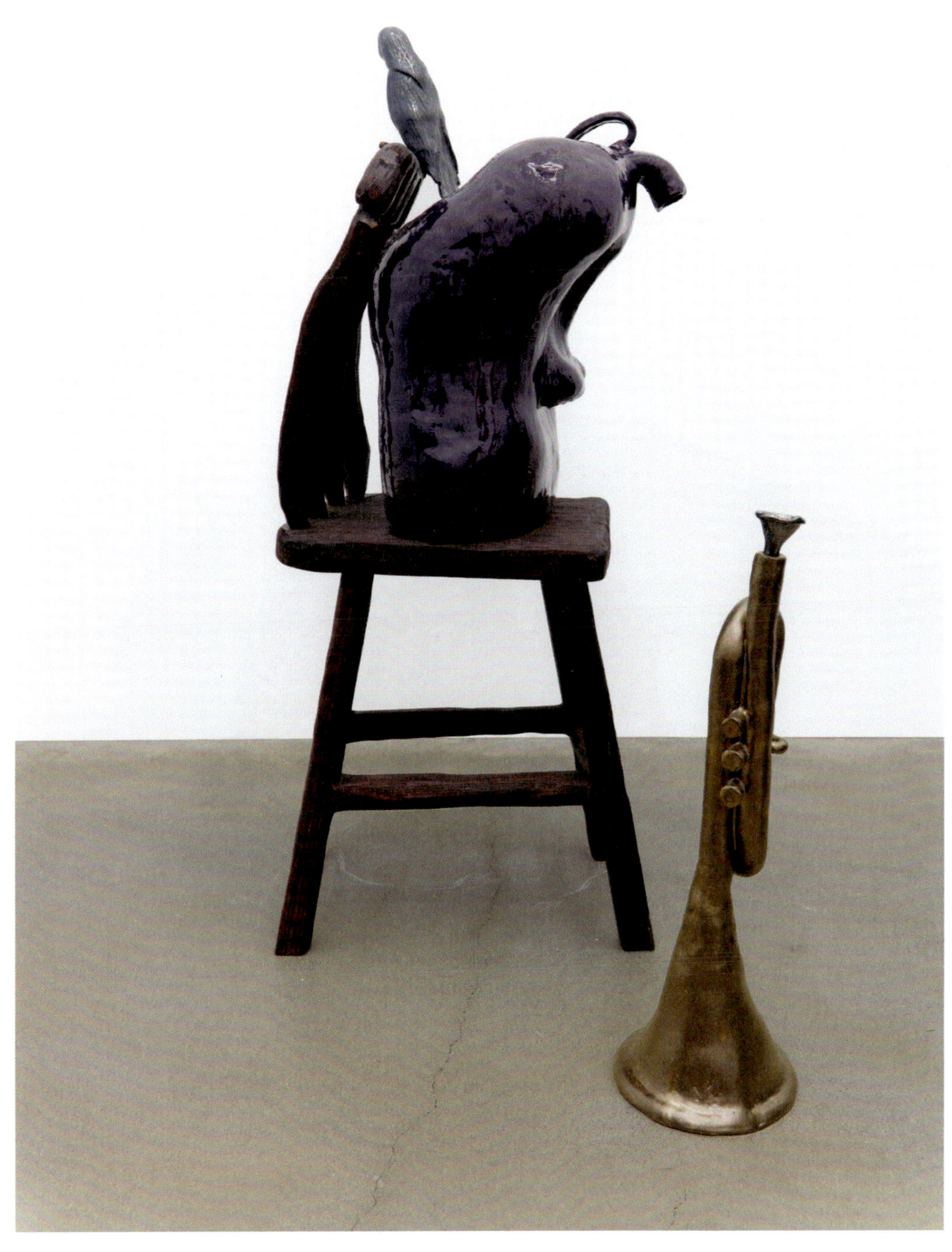

Vibrational pool, 2022. Ceramic, glaze, paint, resin, and wood,
64 × 17 × 18 in. (162.6 × 43.2 × 45.7 cm)

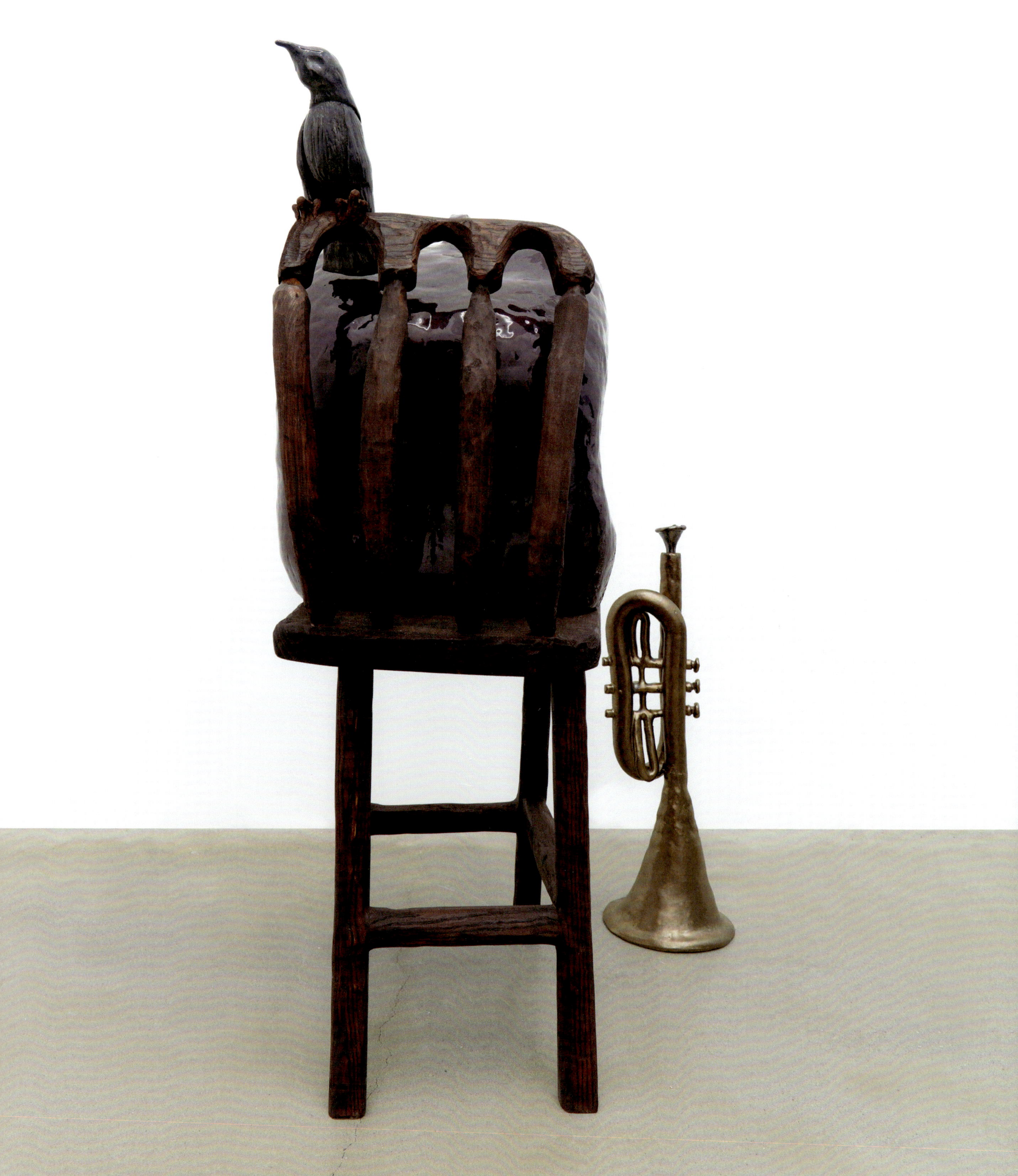

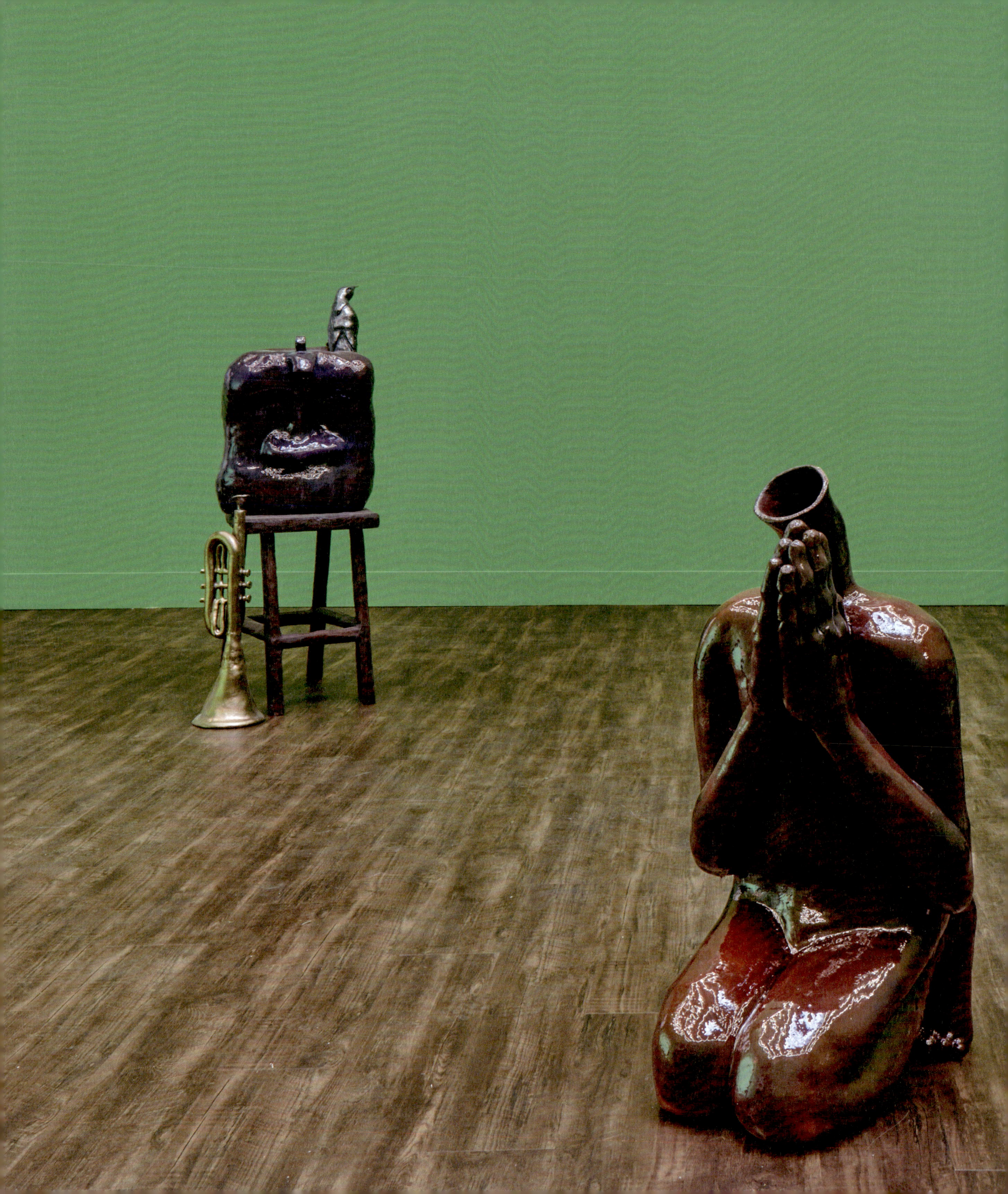

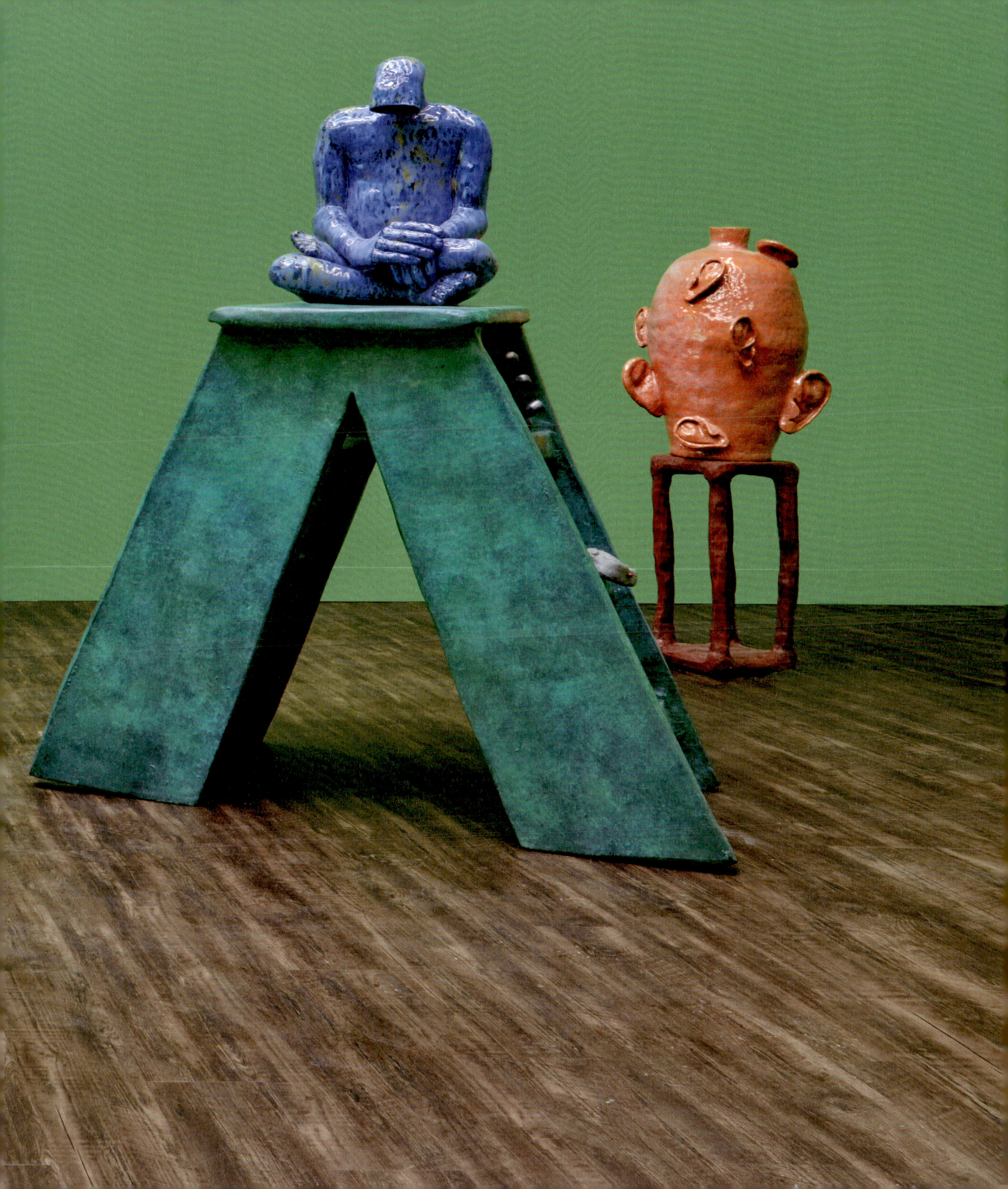

Woody De Othello
in Conversation with
Arlene Shechet

ARLENE SHECHET: I want to say, first off, that my favorite thing about the show is that doorway. Taking the gallery doorway, that big classic white cube opening, and making it narrow and putting a real door on it and then laying down a real/not-real floor—I thought that intervention was genius. That blew my mind because there's so much about passage and also sculpture and movement in a doorway. Immediately, the strangeness of passing through that door felt both right and wrong at the same time—it was a great introduction to the show. It's almost like an Alice in Wonderland thing, like entering into a new belief system. You can tell us anything and we'll believe you. And you did. You told us anything and you had fun. I could feel the energy around that, the intelligence of that move and the thoroughness of that conception.

WOODY DE OTHELLO: There needs to be openness. Looking at your work and looking at your practice, there's so much openness for the viewer and the audience to come into the work and make of it what they want. Your sculptures call so much attention to the body and its relationship to another object. You have to contort and bend and move around to really try and understand what's going on. Then there is so much range and contradiction that exists in a piece, with the texture—some things matte, others shiny, the different materials merging. Or having something at the top of the sculpture that's completely opaque and dense, which has this kind of compression and then these dainty steel legs that are holding it up. I think that contradiction and that clashing is just your own . . . It's as if you're doing something and doing its exact opposite in one piece.

I think that makes for a rich experience as a viewer and somebody who is a fan of sculpture—the way things work in space and in the environment in relation to one's own body. I think that openness is kind of key.

ARLENE SHECHET: Well, I'm going to just write all that down, Woody. I really appreciate it. But I'm going to tell you something: you're my audience. Do you know what I mean? Because you get it.

I never work for a show. I'm always just working, and I always have just worked.

Then, when I have a show, I see what's around and try to edit things into place. The only time I stopped working was at the beginning of the pandemic. I had just had a show that I put a lot into—my first show at Pace. It opened at the end of February 2020. It was supposed to be open for two months. I had a million museum visits scheduled. Ten days later, it closed. Nothing happened. I mean, it wasn't a failure, but it wasn't what it was intended to be.

It wasn't just about that. I also thought, me, my family, we're all going to die because we didn't know what this would be.

WOODY DE OTHELLO: Yeah, that's real. That's very real.

ARLENE SHECHET: So, for the first time in my life, I wasn't able to go to the studio. I could see how I could shut the whole thing down. Everybody around me was so disturbed. My family, who usually said, "Why do you always have to go to the studio?" was now saying, "You need to go to the studio." My assistant was like, "You need to go to the studio." So, I forced myself to do that. There was such power in the quiet of the studio that I could almost forget about everything else, which is a bodily need when you're an artist.

WOODY DE OTHELLO: That's why I go to the studio. Because nothing else matters. My body doesn't matter. Nothing matters. You go in there, and it's peaceful. It's like going to church, it's this transcendental experience. That's the biggest blessing for creative people, or just people who have some type of passion: whatever's going on in the outside world, you have a place, a thing, that's just for you, and it seems like that's a hard thing to come by.

ARLENE SHECHET: *Maybe tomorrow* at Karma reminds me of Buddhist iconography. Tell me about that.

WOODY DE OTHELLO: It all comes from looking at a lot of precolonial African objects. Looking at the forms and understanding why things are kneeling, why things are holding bowls. I was in New York in March and there was a show up at the Met that contextualized African art within Egyptian art, and you see a lot of Egyptian art doing the same things. I thought that was so incredible. So, I've been looking at a lot of those types of references and imagery. They're all very open culturally; they do reference Buddhist poses and stances. But I think part of it is just trying to understand this ancestral note outside of colonization. In looking at a lot of precolonial objects, I've found things that I've never heard about.

That language really makes its way into the sculptures. I'm hoping they're open enough that people across different backgrounds and aspects of life can still relate.

I live in Oakland, which has a rich community, but it's not Los Angeles, it's not New York. Here I can really get into a good studio routine and not be inundated with going to openings and seeing shows. I see things when I want to see them. With studio visits, because I'm in Oakland, I'm not as accessible. So if somebody wants to come here, it's with a very specific intention, not just to fill a Tuesday afternoon.

But I think about time a lot. The thing is, we don't know how much of it we have left. So it's an almost frantic energy of needing to make the thing that I want to make *right now*, so let me get it out of my system as soon as possible. The relationship I have with the studio is based on my understanding of how sacred it is to have time to be in the creative process. It's out of this world. It's almost paranormal. To have these emotions, feelings, images—something going on internally—that need to be transmuted into a physical, actualized thing. That's magic right there. That's alchemy. That's the divine spirit. That's what creation is, right?

I understand how important and special that is, so I don't want to be making work while stressed out or worried about a deadline. My approach to deadlines now is, if I make it, I make it. If it doesn't come out, I'm sorry. It's not like I'm not making things, but sometimes things don't happen, and that's what the studio is.

ARLENE SHECHET: The really important thing about your work is the intimacy. You have to have installation views, but I also try to control my images. Everybody comes in and wants to get the whole view, but I never let them. Also important is your use of color—purple is such an abrasive color.

WOODY DE OTHELLO: I love abrasive colors.

ARLENE SHECHET: I noticed that in your palette, which made me think about how

colors have personalities. You're taking purple and you're making it funny. Color is a whole language. A lot of sculptors don't use color. I feel like a lot of people who play in ceramics come from the painting world, so they love the melted colors, but historically that's really not been a sculpture thing.

WOODY DE OTHELLO: It's tricky to combine color with form, with texture. And your sculptures do all of that. There are so many things to look at on just a formal level. It's mind-blowing. With some of the surfaces and textures, the fact that you even have these things that are opposing forces but are somehow sitting harmoniously together within one

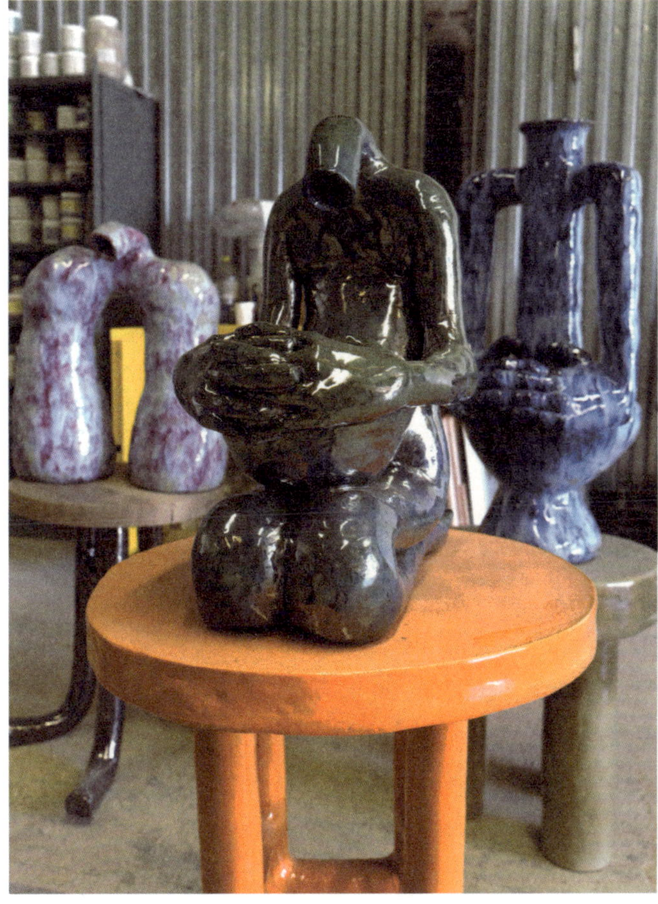

Woody De Othello's studio, Oakland, California, 2022.
Photo: Lacey Lennon

piece—it's a mystery. I think that contradiction makes up a lot of the substance of thinking about and being in the same space as your work. There are a lot of things that bounce back and forth and open your work up. They open me up to add this other relationship to what I'm looking at, it makes for a space that's almost ungrounded. Because everything is in combination, and mixing together. When you're trying to pull the different nuances and textures out, it's so much to take in. It's a lot of information.

ARLENE SHECHET: I appreciate that. The basic ideas of my work are about the fragility of life, and what it's like to be alive and in a body. But at the same time, I think what you're saying is true, which is that you can stand next to my work and appreciate that I had joy, that I'm communicating some kind of joy and excitement, and that I'm sharing it. I like that you don't have to know anything. I feel like that's what art can do; it can communicate that without it being a paragraph. It can communicate, yes, this is a generous act. There's an act of generosity here that I had fun putting together, and I want you to share it with me.

WOODY DE OTHELLO: One of my friends recently asked me, "How do you choose color?" I told them I don't know anything about color theory—contrasting, complementary—I don't know none of that. It's this thing that just kind of lives inside. It's the same with thinking about installation and exhibition and the decisions that I made in the show. In this most recent Karma show, I was randomly making things and then I set aside time for things like needing a couple of punctuations for the wall. You have all these objects on the floor; how, then, does your eye completely move all around the space?

I don't necessarily plan for these decisions, but I have things on hand to help situate the works in space. It's all a dance of how your eye and body move around the room. All these elements come together and I couldn't tell you how or why, it just is the way it is. I'm really learning to trust that first impulse as something to live and die by. Sometimes I'll make the first choice and it won't go the way I wanted, but guess what? I didn't labor over it and there's so much information that comes from just doing the thing instead of sitting around and wondering. It's like, is this even worth the effort? You thought about it. If you have time to do it, just see what the hell happens and go from there. That's how a lot of things are coming together and I'm excited to see what type of weirdness and strangeness and craziness happens in the studio after continuing to work for another decade. It all adds up to this foundation that could be potentially rich and amazing. But that doesn't happen if you do the same thing over and over.

ARLENE SHECHET: That's exactly right. That's why I think it's so much more fun to work than to worry, or overthink, or be precious. To just throw it out. Clay is the ultimate recyclable material. But I throw out a lot of other stuff too. The editing process can be our friend and it sounds like that's something you're very attuned to already.

I'm not going to make you a Buddhist, but working with that idea of fragility and the present moment in that questioning way has a lot to do with contemplative thought from Asia. I don't know a lot about African art but I did read that you were interested in Yoruba practices.

WOODY DE OTHELLO: Yoruba has this undertone of coolness, keeping your head cool under pressure, and this idea of contradictions being able to exist. I grew up Catholic, where the serpent is this evil omen—a sign of the devil on Earth. But in Yoruba, the serpent is the coil between the northern and southern hemispheres. The serpent has the power to take life, but if you admit the right dosage, it also has medicinal powers. So, there's this level of continuous contradiction, things flowing in and out of each other, and people or objects having the potential to be sacred or dangerous—all these things mixing together.

Yoruba is teaching me a lot about accepting things that I can't control, and connecting to the natural world, being around trees and appreciating water and the seasons. There is this rich Black mythology of different deities that I never learned about. I haven't had access to a lot of ancestral knowledge—so much has been erased. This idea of decolonizing—trying to find out what and who I am outside of colonization—is really important to me.

ARLENE SHECHET: How did you originally get turned onto that?

WOODY DE OTHELLO: I read this incredible book by Robert Farris Thompson, *Flash of the Spirit*. And Octavia Butler has these little Yoruba anecdotes in a lot of her novels that come in super sly. In *Lilith's Brood*, the main character's parents wished that she had married a Yoruba man, or in the Parable series, Lauren Olamina's last name comes

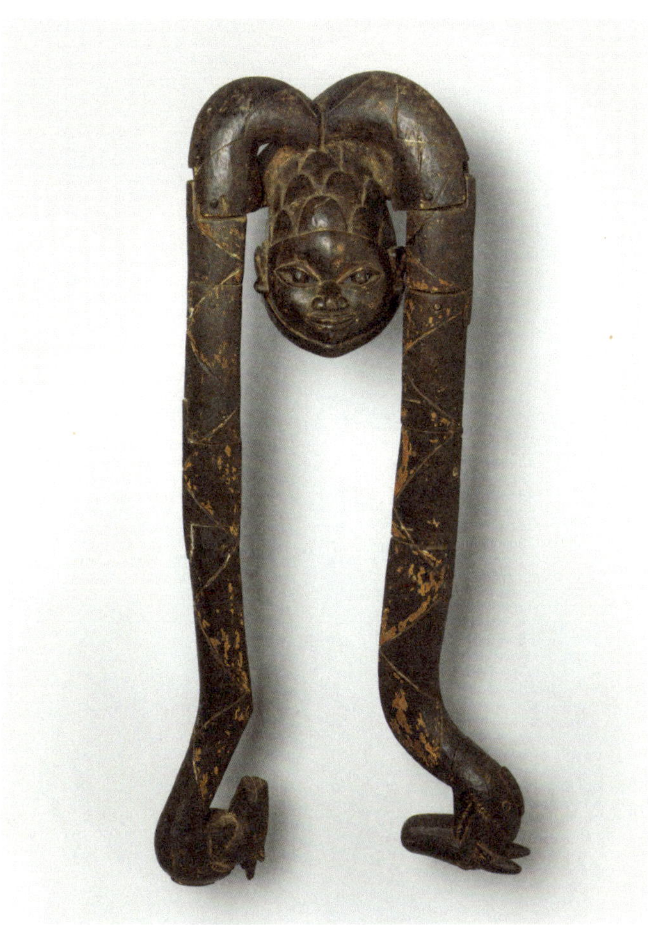

Fagbite Asamu and Falola Edun, Headdress (Gelede), ca. 1930–37. Wood, metal, and pigment, 41 × 19 × 11 in. (104.1 × 48.3 × 27.9 cm). Metropolitan Museum of Art, New York; gift of Roda and Gilbert Graham

from a Yoruba word. Also, through jazz: a lot of jazz musicians name their titles after these super-African things. Max Roach has this song, "Effi." I looked up what "Effi" means, which got me into a whole wormhole. So, it's coming from all different angles.

ARLENE SHECHET: That's very cool. I love that you're embracing the musical at the same time. You've talked about that in a lot of different ways. I'm a huge jazz fan.

WOODY DE OTHELLO: Jazz is a direct connection to the divine. A direct connection

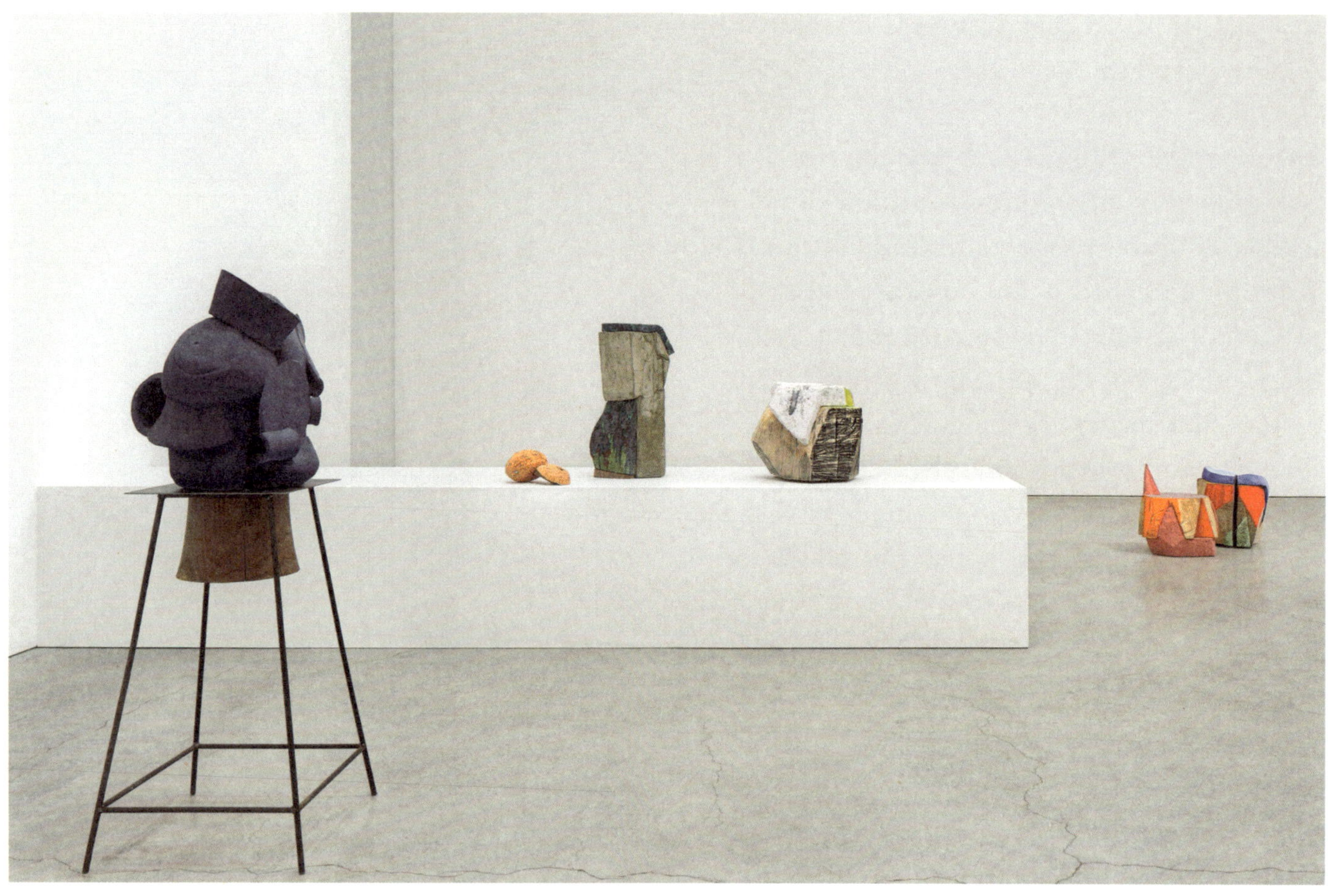

Arlene Shechet, *Turn Up the Bass*, installation view, Sikkema Jenkins & Co., New York, October 13–November 12, 2016. Photo: Phoebe d'Heurle

to being in the moment, trusting your intuition. But then there's this rigor and this practice that allows you to be free with your instrument and with your bandmates, playing together. It's fascinating and incredible. I've been listening to the *Interstellar Space* album by John Coltrane, and it's a piece of work.

Cecil Taylor's *Jazz Advance* also: if I'm in the studio and that's on, I have left the building.

ARLENE SHECHET: That's so good. It's actually great. Well, that whole notion of improvisation is there to feast on. Making work physically, especially sculpture, is like making a move, call and response, and with all art, you make a move and then you pay attention. The thing speaks back to you when you're in the zone with it—you're taking instruction from the artwork. I'm always working on six or seven things at the same time so that I don't get frustrated with anything. I can be like, "Go away!" then move on to another thing.

But what you said speaks to me. I had a show at Jack Shainman Gallery in 2010. I called it *The Sound of It* because it was when I was really understanding jazz on another level. I didn't want to identify what I meant, but everybody started to say, "Are you one of those people who hears voices?" Everybody was taking it so literally.

WOODY DE OTHELLO: But you don't just use your ears to hear stuff.

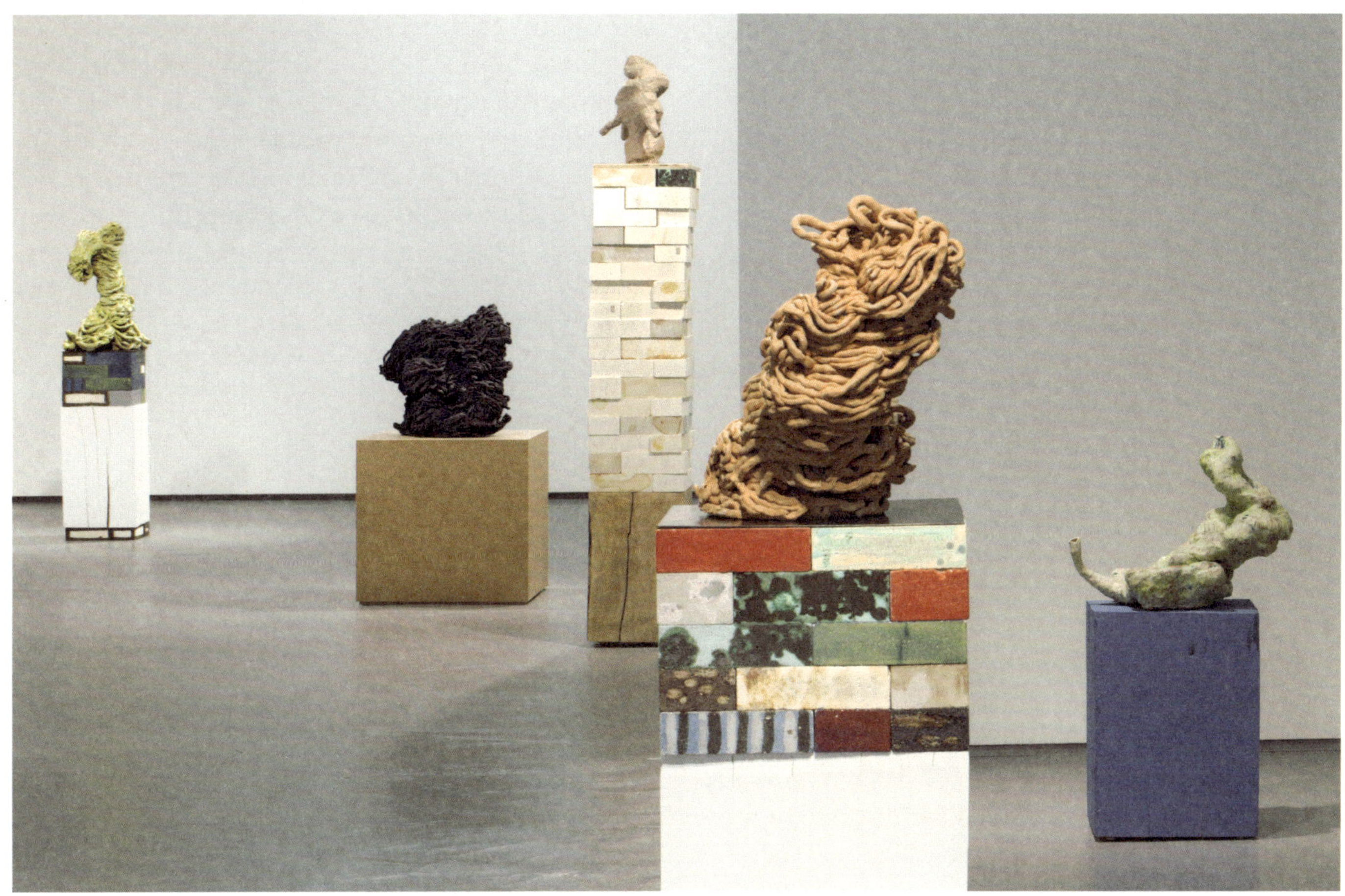

Arlene Shechet, *The Sound of It*, installation view, Jack Shainman Gallery, New York, September 10–October 9, 2010. Photo: Cathy Carver

ARLENE SHECHET: Exactly, that's what I was saying. This thing is emitting sound, if you want to call it sound. It has a voice. What do we mean by having a voice? What do we mean by things speaking to us? It's not just like you and me having this legible conversation. It's way, way, way, way beyond that. That's what those jazz practitioners really understood; they were operating on another plane.

WOODY DE OTHELLO: I appreciate your words, Arlene. I discovered your work in undergrad and it helped me to shape the potential of what ceramic—not even just ceramic sculpture—what art could be. Like, oh, this is ceramics, but it's not ceramics. It's just sculpture. Art is something else on its own. Your work really gives me the energy to want to try and cultivate something that feels free and expansive and void of other comparisons.

WOODY DE OTHELLO: It definitely reached me in South Florida.

ARLENE SHECHET: That's a beautiful thing. I'm so thrilled that we got to have this conversation, and I can't wait for your next trip to New York—we'll go hear some music.

WOODY DE OTHELLO: I'm definitely ringing your line. That's going to be amazing.

111

This book is published in conjunction with

Woody De Othello
Maybe tomorrow
September 24–November 5, 2022

Karma
22 East 2nd Street
New York, New York

© 2023 Karma Books, New York

Edition of 1,000

All works by Woody De Othello
© Woody De Othello

Printed and bound by die Keure

Pages 25–27, 38–39, 46–47, 52–53, 58–59,
72–73, 78–79, 84–85, 97, 102–103: Woody De
Othello, *Maybe tomorrow*, installation views,
Karma, September 24–November 5, 2022.
Photos: Max Lee-Russell

ISBN 978-1-949172-96-6